"Whether breaking tackles, dancing with the stars, or building his businesses, Emmitt has always striven to be excellent in all he does each day. Readers of this book will learn just what it takes to be a champion in every aspect of life, including the all-important areas of faith and family."

BISHOP T. D. JAKES
Senior pastor of The Potter's House of Dallas and CEO of TDJ Enterprises

"When Emmitt came to the Cowboys, he told his teammates that when he retired, he would be the NFL's all-time leading rusher. I watched him pursue his dream with relentless determination, overcoming adversity on several occasions and never once wavering from his goal. If anybody is qualified to write a book about daring to dream, it is my teammate and my friend Emmitt Smith."

DARYL JOHNSTON
Former Cowboys fullback and commentator on NFL on Fox

"I may have helped Emmitt Smith become a great ballroom dancer, but he taught me about living like a champion in all aspects of life, respecting yourself and others, and always reaching higher to make the most of your talents while using them to benefit those around you. This book is a great gift to us all, and so is Emmitt Smith."

CHERYL BURKE
Champion of Dancing with the Stars

GAME ON

FIND YOUR PURPOSE—PURSUE YOUR DREAM

EMMITT SMITH

Hall of Fame Running Back and Dancing with the Stars *Champion*

Tyndale House Publishers, Inc.

Carol Stream, Illinois

Library of Congress Cataloging-in-Publication Data

Smith, Emmitt, date.
  Game on : find your purpose—pursue your dream / Emmitt Smith.
    p. cm.
  ISBN 978-1-4143-4981-7 (hc)
  1. Success—Religious aspects—Christianity. 2. Self-actualization (Psychology)—Religious aspects—Christianity. 3. Dreams—Religious aspects—Christianity. 4. Smith, Emmitt, date—Religion. I. Title.
  BV4598.3.S65 2011
  248.4—dc23   2011024186

Printed in the United States of America

17   16   15   14   13   12   11
7   6   5   4   3   2   1

I dedicate this book to my wife, Pat, and my children, E.J., Jasmin, Rheagen, Skylar, and Elijah, for inspiring and supporting me in whatever I do. I love you, and I'm always there for you!

I also dedicate this book to my parents, Mary and Emmit Smith Jr. They built the foundation on which I stand today, and whatever I accomplish in life is the result of their abiding love and wise guidance. To my brothers, Erik and Emory, and my sisters, Marsha and Connie— thank you, too, for your love and support over the years. Also to my late brother, Emil—you may be gone, but you're not forgotten.

CONTENTS

WELCOME TO *GAME ON*

I've written this book to share with you the many lessons I've learned as well as the mistakes I've made in my life and my career. I hope what I have to say will help you pursue and achieve your dreams in whatever game you play.

I am often asked to speak to students, corporate leaders, and organizations because of my successful journey from a Pensacola public housing development to the Pro Football Hall of Fame—and there was a little televised dancing championship somewhere in there too. I enjoy telling my story, even as I am still writing its latest chapters in pursuit of opportunities in business, sports, and entertainment.

What I hope you'll remember as you read is that I didn't begin life as a Hall of Fame running back or a television celebrity. There were many who doubted I would ever make it in the National Football League (NFL). You will have your doubters too. When they come around, tell them what I told mine:

Game on!

I have always been determined to achieve my dreams no matter what anyone else might say or think. I was willing to do whatever it took to become the person I needed to be so I could claim the goals I'd set for myself. You can do the same.

Like me, you won't do it alone. My faith, my family, and my friends have made a huge difference in my life. I stood on the shoulders of many wonderful and helpful people when I accepted my Hall of Fame award. They believed in me because they saw I believed in myself and was committed to being a champion.

Where you start doesn't matter. It's where you finish that counts. And how you end up in this life depends on what you do every day to accomplish your goals. Each day is a step toward building a legacy, a life of meaning and fulfillment. I didn't break the NFL rushing record by running 18,355 yards in one game. I did it by setting the goal to gain at least four yards on every carry of every NFL game.

And I didn't achieve every goal I set for myself—at least on the first try. Sometimes I fell short. You will too. But sometimes I exceeded my goal—or I kept trying until I achieved it.

You will do that too.

If you put your heart into it as well as your mind and body, I believe you will have a championship-caliber life. This book offers a practical, step-by-step plan based on my personal experience. Here's a quick summary of what it takes:

- *Step 1.* Envision what you want, and then dream of the best possible life.
- *Step 2.* Turn your dreams into goals, and pursue your highest possible purpose as defined by God's gifts within you.

- *Step 3.* Build a strong moral character based on your own values and principles.
- *Step 4.* Pursue your dreams and highest purpose with unrelenting commitment and unfailing consistency.
- *Step 5.* Be courageous even when faced with the worst of your fears and the greatest of challenges.
- *Step 6.* Seize and create opportunities that match up with your long-term goals and principles.
- *Step 7.* Build a championship team of supporters, role models, and mentors.
- *Step 8.* Maintain a winning attitude even during setbacks and defeats.
- *Step 9.* Make wise decisions, and reduce risk to keep yourself on track.
- *Step 10.* Return God's favor with your heart open to him and your hand open to your fellow human beings.

This plan does not offer a magic pill or a secret formula. I don't make any claims that these are original concepts. Most are taught in the Bible and in the writings of both ancient and modern philosophers. They have been tested over time and in the lives of many, and they have certainly made a difference in my own life.

But simply reading the steps won't result in a life-changing transformation. The rewards you reap will be directly related to the effort you make in following these steps and making them a part of your life.

But don't worry. You can do it. I know you can.

Game on!

CHAPTER 1

CLAIM YOUR DREAMS

If there were prophets among you,
I, the LORD, would reveal myself in visions.
I would speak to them in dreams.

NUMBERS 12:6, NLT

BEFORE I'D EVER SCORED A TOUCHDOWN for the University of Florida Gators or the Dallas Cowboys, I crossed the goal line untouched hundreds and hundreds of times. I did it as a small boy in the park across the street from my grandmother's house in Pensacola, Florida. My field of dreams was a little park called Malaga Square—though back then I never knew those raggedy two acres even had a name. It was just a sparse patch of ground, but it gave a kid from the housing projects room to run.

And run I did.

My cousins usually played football with me there, but often I'd be the first on the field. While waiting for the others to show up, I'd throw the football into the air and let my imagination run as far as it would take me:

There's the kickoff. The football is in the air, and Emmitt Smith catches it at the five-yard line. He runs to the left sideline and makes it to the twenty, but here comes a tackler. He spins away, and now Emmitt Smith turns into Jim Brown bulling through another pair of tacklers. A cut to his right, and he's Tony Dorsett sprinting to the far sideline. He hurdles a defender, and now he's Walter Payton, weaving through the defense and sprinting toward the goal line. He's at the thirty, the twenty, the ten . . . Emmitt Smith scores a touchdown!

The record book says that in my NFL career, I ran for 164 touchdowns and 18,355 yards, surpassing Walter Payton's all-time leading rushing record of 16,726 yards. I'm here to tell you I ran for a lot more touchdowns and a lot more yards at old Malaga Square. As I sprinted down the field of my boyhood dreams, I'd transform into each of my football heroes one after the other, imitating each player's signature moves.

I could hear the roar of the crowd with every cut back, every spin, and every fresh burst of speed. My creative mind was racing even faster than my legs. I was a boy at play, but something far more important and lasting was taking place in that park.

A child was running after his dreams on the power of his imagination.

In a sense, I've never stopped running.

And I've *never* stopped dreaming.

A CHAMPIONSHIP-LEVEL DREAMER

I believe there are great things in store for my life and yours, too. Greatness is not reserved for VIPs. Happiness and fulfillment are not limited commodities. The question is, are you willing to do whatever it takes to become the person you need to be, to achieve the life you want to live?

If you are happy right where you are, that's fine. But if you feel that God has more in store for you, then I encourage you to step into your workout gear and read on. The first step in this process is to trust in your vision for that better life and dare to dream big.

The Bible says in Numbers 12:6,

If there were prophets among you,
I, the LORD, would reveal myself in visions.
I would speak to them in dreams. (NLT)

Wiser men than I have commented over the centuries about the awesome power of our visions, our dreams, and the human imagination. Poets, philosophers, writers, great military and political leaders, and probably even a rap star or two have noted that our visions and dreams are the pathways and portals to a better life. That has certainly been true for me, and it can be true for you, too.

We are all born naked into this world, but each of us is fully clothed in potential. Every one of us possesses unique gifts that we must embrace and develop to the fullest. But we can't do that if we don't have a vision. We can't do that if we're afraid to dream.

I'm not referring to idle daydreams or grandiose, self-centered imaginings. I'm talking about the way you visualize or picture the life you yearn for, the life that God is calling you to. Having vision means picturing in your mind what it will be like and how you will achieve it and build upon it. Dreaming means "rehearsing" what you see, playing it over and over in your mind until it becomes as real to you as your life right now.

The two go together. Vision gets the dreams started. Dreaming employs your God-given imagination to reinforce the vision. Both are part of something I believe is absolutely necessary to building the life of a champion, a winner, a person of high character who is consistently at the top of whatever game he or she is in.

I was a championship-level dreamer as a boy. When we were riding in our parents' car through the nicer neighborhoods of Pensacola, my sister and brothers and I would spot our favorite big homes and claim them:

"That brick one's mine!"

"The house with the big front porch is mine!"

Other times we'd sit on the curb in our own neighborhood and claim the nicest cars passing by.

"Oh, that Mustang is mine!"

"That Cadillac is mine!"

What can I say? We were just crazy kids. But even though we came from a low-income family, we dared to dream that anything was possible for us, anything was within our reach if we were willing to work for it and keep reaching for it.

Winning isn't something that just happens to you on the field when the whistle blows or the crowd roars. Winning is something that is built physically and mentally every day that you train and every night that you dream. The victories we achieve, then, are the result of the vision that fuels our commitment to making our dreams a reality.

THE POWER OF DREAMS

As children in a middle- to low-income family, my brothers and sister and I had fewer advantages than most. So my journey offers good evidence that when you dare to claim your dreams and always strive to do your best, nothing can hold you back.

Your dream may not be anything like mine. You may have no interest at all in playing sports or developing a business. Your idea of a "better life" may involve making more money so you can help your family . . . or simplifying your lifestyle so you can live on *less* money and have more free time. You may have an inner yearning to paint or to travel the world or to establish an AIDS clinic in Africa or to retire to the mountains.

Your dreams will vary with your interests, your desires, your stage of life, and your receptiveness to God's leading in your life. But until you dare to claim these dreams—to acknowledge them to yourself and to others and to rehearse them in your mind and heart—you will never get started. Your dreams provide the energy you need to move forward and keep striving to do and be your best.

My life, like yours, did not come with any guarantees of success. At five feet nine inches tall, I was not exactly the prototype for the modern running back. Many scouts thought I was too small and too slow to play beyond high school. The doubters were proven wrong because they could not measure the reach of my imagination or the size of my heart. My ability to dream, to develop vision for my life and then make it happen through commitment and consistent effort, sent me soaring to heights beyond anyone's expectations—except my own.

After playing football in high school and then in three record-breaking seasons at the University of Florida, I entered the draft after my junior year and was selected by the Dallas Cowboys. I went on to thrive for fifteen years in the NFL, won a few Super Bowls, broke a few records, and in August of 2010, I am honored to say, I was inducted into the Pro Football Hall of Fame.

Reporters and sports broadcasters who covered the induction ceremony again noted my lack of size and speed, but one thing they gave me credit for was having great vision on the field. Many showed game films of me running and stopping or cutting just as two defenders descended on me, causing them either to miss me altogether or to run into each other as I charged on toward the goal line. I loved it when they hit each other instead of me!

I do have exceptional peripheral vision, but my inner vision is even better—and over the long haul that's what really has made the difference in my life. The Bible says in Proverbs 29:18, "Where there is no vision, the people perish" (KJV). Your inner vision, your ability to picture a better life for yourself and to pursue it, can save your life—and elevate it too.

As a boy and even later, I would first "see" myself achieving something—like playing college and professional football or having a career in the construction industry—and then my vision would drive my dreams. In my dreams, I would see myself fulfilling that vision over and over until I believed in my heart and soul that I could make my dreams happen in reality.

That ability to "see" helped me on the football field, too. I had a sort of inner big screen that allowed me to "see" changes in coverage. I could usually look at a defense and sense where the hole would be, regardless of where the play was called. Admittedly, this process became more challenging in the NFL, where defenses are far more sophisticated than in high school and college. In high school I could often point my fullback to where I felt a hole would be just prior to the snap. Every now and then, just to test this inner vision, I'd run at the hole I'd seen in my mind's eye with my real eyes shut. (Kids, don't try this at home!)

I've heard many other athletes describe similar experiences in which they envision themselves reacting to a situation before it actually happens. Quarterbacks, running backs, and receivers often talk about seeing a play unfold in their minds split seconds before it happens on the field. Some of this comes with the repetitive training that athletes go through. We run plays over and over and over again in practice, and then we watch them on film. Those plays keep running in our minds even after we go home. I know at night my mind would keep running the Cowboys' plays over and over until they became embedded in my subconscious and my responses on the field became instinctive.

Still, some of the things that have shown up on my mind's inner big screen are difficult to explain. Even scientists admit that our understanding of the human brain and its workings is still very limited. I do believe that most of us, if not all of us, have a degree of intuition, a so-called sixth sense—the ability to see in our mind's eye beyond what our own eyes tell us. I experienced that sort of vision in my athletic career, and I've also had it in my business life, when I would look at a vacant lot and "see" a commercial building on it with thriving stores and businesses.

I've worked at developing that sixth sense. It's a great asset, a gift of God, but only if you trust and then act on it. Creating a vision for your life is an essential first step, but your dreams will live only in your imagination unless you pursue them purposefully and relentlessly.

NOT JUST ANY DREAM

Having a vision for something better and dreaming of fulfilling that vision are important keys to creating the life God wants for you. Some people wander in the darkness. My dreams gave me a lighted path. Holding a vision of a better life in mind also served to motivate me because I saw that there were greater possibilities awaiting me. When you have a vision of yourself doing great things, that vision excites you and, in the process, prepares you for greatness.

Vision also keeps you hungry. When I won one rushing title, I was happy but not fully satisfied, because I saw more for myself. I wanted to win as many rushing titles as possible because I had noticed that my rushing titles and Super Bowl victories tended to coincide. I stayed hungry because I wanted to help Dallas win more Super Bowls.

So welcome your visions of a better life, dare to dream of what your heart deeply desires, and then pursue those dreams with all your heart, mind, body, and soul.

Know that whatever you lack, God will provide—given, of course, that you've opened your heart to what God wants for your life.

That's important, because it's a mistake to assume God will automatically support *anything* you happen to want or desire or picture for yourself. After all, not all dreams are from God. The people who brought my ancestors as slaves to America had a vision for all the money they could make with that particular "business venture." I don't believe God supported that. So if you want a truly winning life—something more than just "making it" in the world—it's always important to check your dreams and desires against God's standards of right and wrong.

At the same time, I don't believe you actually need a specific vision from the Lord—like a voice in a dream or handwriting on the wall—in order to claim your dreams and go for them. Many of our dreams, especially when we're children, are simply part of the package God made when he put us on earth. They grow out of our interests and talents and yearnings and imaginations, combined with the circumstances we find ourselves in. They don't have to involve a direct revelation to be from God.

That was true for me. I'm not a psychic. I have no superpowers. I was just a kid who had faith in my Lord and Savior, Jesus Christ, and in the power of the dreams he gave me. But those dreams were what propelled me toward the person I needed to become, the life I believe God had in mind for me.

Whatever your circumstances are right now, no matter how hard you have it, no matter how many challenges you face, you can move to a better life if you have a vision for where you want to go. When your vision is planted inside you by God, he will help you do whatever it takes to make it a reality.

I believe in the power of dreams because I've had several incredible incidents in my life in which my wildest dreams became wonderful realities. Let me give you a couple of examples.

VISION NUMBER ONE

I was seven years old, sprawled on the floor in our Pensacola living room and watching a Sunday afternoon football game on television with some relatives and my father, Emmit Jr. (He spells his name with one *t* instead of two.) The Dallas Cowboys were one of the teams playing. I liked their uniforms. I liked the way they played the game. At one point about halfway through it, I turned to my father and said, "Pop, one day I'm going to play professional football, and I'm going to play for the Dallas Cowboys."

That bold statement resulted from a vision that fueled a dream. I couldn't hold a football in one hand at that point, but I was already getting a mental picture of what I wanted to do in my life. I wasn't aware at the time that my father had been a very good football player, so where did the vision come from? Was it merely my desire—or was it my desire coupled with God's plan for my life? I can't say for sure, but I do believe God has unique ways of revealing and fulfilling his plans for us. My professional football career serves as a prime example of that.

VISION NUMBER TWO

Let's move ahead to my senior season in high school. I was named the Gatorade Player of the Year, and part of the prize included two tickets for the Super Bowl, which would be played that year at the Rose Bowl in Pasadena, California. As a Christmas present, I invited Johnny Nichols, the quarterback on our team and my best friend, to go with me to the biggest game of the year.

Think about all that had to happen to put my best friend and me—two kids from the wrong side of the tracks in Pensacola, Florida—side by side in the crowd at the Super Bowl. If God's hand wasn't hard at work to pull that off, well, I don't know what to tell you. Nor can I tell you what made me say this to Johnny during the game: "You know what? One day I want to play in a Super Bowl in this stadium."

At that point there were a lot of people who didn't think I had the slightest chance of becoming a starter at college or even playing at the Division I level. How could I be so bold as to say out loud to a good friend—one with a very good memory—that one day I'd be an NFL player in a Super Bowl at the Rose Bowl? That's crazy. And Johnny may have said exactly that when the words slipped out of my mouth.

DREAM MACHINE

I've come to realize that the greatest gift God has given me, besides his love and the love of my family, is this gift of vision—the ability to see beyond where I am to where I want to be. I've often talked about that in news articles and interviews—mostly as it pertains to football. Rarely have I shared with anyone the other dreams that began when I was playing in that Pensacola park across the street from my grandmother's house.

When we were still in the early years of grade school and not playing football, baseball, or basketball, my brothers and friends and I would sit on the bare, dusty ground of the park with Popsicle sticks in our hands. Using the dirt as our drawing board, we'd map out entire neighborhoods. This was way before iPads—not that our families could have afforded them anyway. So we were left to our imaginations and wooden Popsicle sticks to dig out roads for our Matchbox cars.

I wasn't just interested in the cars, though. I always drew an outline of the home I wanted to have one day. My dream homes were very different from the segregated apartment buildings we lived in. They were big *Leave It to Beaver* houses with generous yards and white picket fences—like the places we saw when we ventured across the tracks to the more affluent areas of Pensacola.

Those better, safer neighborhoods weren't really that far away, but they almost seemed like they were from another universe. Yet I dared to dream I could live in one someday, unlikely as it seemed. Maybe I could even design good places for other people to live. That was the beginning of yet another dream, one that I'm still working on as I build my construction and real-estate businesses.

I encourage you to dream that way too, to embrace even your unlikely visions—and not just for your own sake, but for the sake of others as well.

TRICKLE-DOWN DREAMS

My pastor and spiritual guide, Bishop T. D. Jakes, has said that if you and I allow our dreams to die, everyone suffers. It's not just the individual who loses out. Just think of the "trickle down" benefits we've all received thanks to great teachers who've pursued their dreams, not to mention the doctors, nurses, firefighters, police officers, scientists, coaches, and religious and community leaders who have contributed to the betterment of our lives.

When you don't fulfill your highest potential, everyone who might have benefited from your gifts loses too. The Wright brothers struggled for years to develop their first successful flying machine. If they'd given up, the whole world might have lost out. The vision, hard work, and persistence of the Wrights and other aviation pioneers led to the creation of entire industries that today provide millions of jobs and access to places around the world. We have all benefited from dreamers who became doers, those who didn't let failures and setbacks deter them.

If I had not followed first my dream to be a professional

> Winning isn't something that just happens to you on the field when the whistle blows or the crowd roars. Winning is something that is built physically and mentally every day that you train and every night that you dream.

athlete and then to be a real-estate developer and builder, I might never have been able to create a charitable foundation with my wife, Pat, that has provided college scholarships and other assistance to scores of young people. In sports I earned the capital to invest in my own business, and in business I will continue to earn the respect of the business community while earning a living and helping our charitable efforts. But all of that started as a dream that almost seemed impossible—except to me.

My parents and my brothers and sisters operated a store selling my football memorabilia in Pensacola for several years, adding to the family income. Many sportswear vendors benefited from my football career too. Although my real-estate development and construction businesses are just being established, one day I hope to provide jobs and financial security for many who work for me and for others who work at the hotels, retail stores, and other facilities we develop.

The first big development project my real-estate company took on was a $190 million hotel and retail site on a prominent street corner in New York City's famed Harlem neighborhood. This project appealed to me because Harlem has historically been an African American neighborhood, and the people who live there have not had access to the same kinds of stores and restaurants that other New Yorkers enjoy. We also negotiated with the labor unions so that local residents would have priority for at least half the construction jobs. The project will create many jobs both during the construction phase and long after the building is done.

As I write this, we are still in the early stages of the Harlem project, but my goal is to build the hotel atop a retail area that will serve the unmet needs of residents. I'd like to have a nice grocery store in the building, for example. It would be a privilege for me, as someone who grew up in a small southern town, to bring something of value to a legendary big-city neighborhood like Harlem.

That thought really hit home one day during the planning stages of our Harlem project. My partners and I met for lunch at Sylvia's, Harlem's landmark soul-food restaurant. When we walked in, several Sylvia's regulars looked up and said, "Welcome, neighbor!" They understood that if I made my business dream become a reality, it would have a positive impact on their community. Their recognition of that and their warm welcome made me all the more determined to bring something of value to their community.

When you dare to dream and then pursue your dreams, you, too, can make an impact far beyond what you might imagine. If you can embrace that thought, you can use it for motivation to take your personal vision and make it a reality.

DREAM BIG FOR A BETTER LIFE

The great thing about believing in the power of your dreams and pursuing them is that even if your income is limited and your circumstances problematic, you can dream as big as the richest man on earth. I grew up in a large and supportive family, which is a major advantage in many ways, but my parents had to work very hard to keep us all fed and clothed. Our Pensacola wasn't the one you see on the tourism brochures. We had no views of the white, sandy beaches or the Gulf of Mexico from the windows of our rented apartment at 138 Attucks Court.

Ours wasn't the worst housing project in town, though we did have rats like I've never seen since. Some of them were as big as cats. And there were even larger predators prowling around if you took the wrong path or knocked on the wrong door. Shootings, stabbings, drug dealers, drunks, and prostitutes were part of our daily environment.

One day when I was about eleven, my friend Robert and I were on our way to football practice. While we walked down the street, a car pulled up alongside us. There was a white man behind the wheel. I thought he was lost and looking for directions, so when he gestured to me to come over, I went. Robert followed a little behind me. (Kids, don't be naive like me—stay away from strangers!)

"Kid, can you shoot me up?" the man said.

I had no idea what that meant.

"What?" I said.

He held up a hypodermic needle and gave me a crazy look. "Shoot me up?"

Robert showed me some real speed that day. He was a block ahead of me before I even turned to run, but I caught up pretty fast. I ran from that man and the wasted life he represented, but I'm sad to say there were others in the neighborhood who followed his dead-end path. Some of our friends fell into the traps of drugs, alcohol, crime, and violence. We weren't better than them in any way. Most of them were good people with their own gifts and talents, and I'm deeply saddened that they were unable to break free from their circumstances.

Looking back on my childhood, I realize how fortunate my sister (Marsha), my brothers (Erik and Emory), and I were. Sure, we lived in the projects and ate government-surplus cheese and powdered milk, but so did most of the kids we knew. And we were blessed with one true luxury—two loving, hardworking, and responsible parents and two whole sets of grandparents who served as our backup mothers and fathers.

I can hardly express to you what a great blessing it was to be surrounded with all that love and support. Our parents and grand-parents instilled in us a strong faith and the sense that we could do anything we wanted with our lives if we were willing to do the work required. They gave us permission to dream and supported our efforts, and that made a huge difference.

Even with that advantage, I am still living proof that where you are and what you have does not have to determine who you are or where you are going. And by the way, that's true of people without intact and supportive homes too. I know plenty of people from divorced families who have managed to find other guides and encouragers and to rise above those circumstances.

My point is that what lies around you does not have to live within you. How you begin life is not nearly as important as how you end up. You can rise above whatever tries to hold you down as long as you stay focused on your dreams.

RISING ABOVE

In my first run in my first NFL game, I was tackled after gaining just one yard. It was not the beginning I had in mind. Fifteen years later, I retired with the most career rushing yards in the history of the game, three Super Bowl rings, four NFL rushing titles, nine Pro Bowl selections, a Super Bowl Most Valuable Player (MVP) award, and an NFL MVP award. I'd say that's a pretty decent way to end a career, wouldn't you?

You have to agree that the way I began my NFL career had little impact on how I finished. What's true for me can be true for you. Maybe you grew up on the wrong side of the tracks too. Maybe you are in a tough position right now. You may not be happy with where life has taken you so far. You may have suffered in the housing crisis, lost a job, failed in a relationship, or received a depressing diagnosis. Hard times may have piled up at your door, and you may be discouraged in your situation. Yet I'm here to tell you that if you can look up, you can get up.

The recession of 2006–2009 slowed my efforts to build a commercial real-estate and construction business, but I believe I'll eventually achieve my goals in this area as well. I walk in confidence, knowing I have the same burning in my heart to succeed in this arena that I had on the football field. If this isn't God's plan for my life, I trust he'll let me know. In the meantime, I'm wholeheartedly committed to living out this vision and rising above the setbacks I've encountered.

Given my belief in God and in the power of my dreams, you probably won't be surprised to learn that one of my favorite Bible stories is the one about Joseph, the most favored son of Jacob—the one they called "the dreamer."

Yes, this is *the* Joseph, the boy who had incredible dreams. His doting father gave Joseph a beautiful coat of many colors—a dream coat—that incited the jealousy and wrath of his half brothers. When Jacob interpreted one of these dreams to mean that the family would one day bow before Joseph, the other brothers threw Joseph into a pit. Later they sold him to traders who in turn sold him as a slave in Egypt, telling their father he'd been killed by wild beasts. They even displayed his torn and bloodied dream coat as evidence.

Joseph was sold to Potiphar, the captain of the palace guard. When Joseph spurned the advances of Potiphar's wife, she claimed that Joseph had attacked her. He was thrown into prison, but even there God showed him favor, and Joseph was put in charge of the other prisoners. When two prisoners had dreams, Joseph interpreted them and the interpretations came true. Word that Joseph had the ability to interpret dreams eventually reached the pharaoh. The pharaoh sent for Joseph, whose dream interpretations helped save Egypt from a famine. Joseph became a respected leader in Egypt, second only to Pharaoh. And later, when his famine-stricken family came looking for food, Joseph not only forgave his brothers and was reunited with his loving father, but he was also able to keep his entire family and the people of Egypt from starving. By the end, it was clear that Joseph's dreams had been prophecies sent to him by God.

That's my *Cliff's Notes* version of Joseph's story, which is not only in the Bible (Genesis), but has been retold many times in plays, movies, and song. Once again, it is not where you start but where you finish that counts. Joseph's brothers sold him into slavery out of jealousy, yet because of God's favor—and the power of his dreams—he rose to a position of wealth and power and, to his credit, he forgave his brothers and saved them from the famine.

I love this story because it confirms how God can use dreams to lift us out of our circumstances, to help us rise above whatever threatens to hold us back. I was never bold enough to think that my dreams were prophecies sent from God, but I did come to believe that even my wildest dreams might have been planted in my imagination and my heart by God's hand. He wanted me to envision a better life so I would develop the talents he had given me and put them to their highest use.

You and I have no control over where we begin our lives, but we do have the power to determine where we end up. How do you exercise that power? It takes focus, commitment, discipline, and thoughtful decision making. Our success on this earth—the happiness we achieve, the fulfillment we find, the relationships we build—all are the result of the choices we make every minute and every hour and every day in our lives.

You can choose to be a victim. You can decide that you've had enough, that life is unfair and just too hard. You can hit the bottle, do drugs, and embrace despair. Those options are all available. Or you can envision a better life and pursue it.

I encourage you to dare to dream and to act upon those dreams. We are all made in God's image. We are anointed. You would not be walking this earth if the Lord did not have a plan for you. The challenges God sends your way are in direct proportion to the blessings he has in store for you if you refuse to give up, if you strive to put your gifts to his highest purpose, and—this is important!—if you keep yourself open to his guidance along the way.

LIGHT FOR YOUR PATH

I spent most of my final months in high school talking about how great it would be to move to Gainesville, enroll at the University of Florida, and play football as a Gator. I was excited until the time came to actually walk out the door. Then my perspective changed. I swear I felt homesick before I'd stepped outside.

By that time we were living in a brick house my father had built right behind his parents' home, literally in their backyard. He'd wanted to be close to them because my grandmother, Erma Lee Smith, was partially paralyzed and in a wheelchair. I had often stayed with her and cared for her, so she and I were close. I walked across the yard to say good-bye to her before driving to Gainesville five hours to the east.

On this day, my grandmother had prepared something special for me to take to college. Little did she know it would accompany me for the rest of my life.

I found her sitting in her chair. It was parked in its usual spot, next to a table and couch and in front of a window where she could watch us come and go from our house in the backyard.

"Get my Bible," she said.

I picked up her worn King James Bible, but before I could hand it to her she said, "Read Proverbs 3:5-6."

"Trust in the LORD with all thine heart; and lean not unto thine own understanding. In all thy ways acknowledge him, and he shall direct thy paths." I read that passage out loud to her, and at that point I studied and memorized it. Then my grandmother said, "Always remember that verse." I thanked her, gave her a hug, and walked out to the driveway to leave.

It's a five-hour drive from Pensacola to Gainesville under normal conditions, but it seemed even longer that day. I was a typical eighteen-year-old guy going off to college. There were many things on my mind that day, and I'd have even more on my mind in the days that followed. And I have to admit that I wasn't in a spiritual frame of mind every minute of every day and night that I was away from my family. I am a much better Christian today than I was then, though I did belong to a Bible study group in college.

But no matter where I was spiritually, or physically, I always carried Proverbs 3:5-6 with me. I held on to my grandmother's verse when I was homesick, hurt, or discouraged. Whenever I needed some comfort, it comforted me.

I didn't talk about it to anyone, but Proverbs 3:5-6 was like one of those night-lights you buy for your kids so that if they are scared or worried in the dark, they can look to that small glowing light for comfort and reassurance. I would even read it or recite it to myself before football games to calm and assure myself. It comforted me to think that I had a path, a destiny, and that even though I might not always understand why something happened or where it was taking me, God knew the where and the why.

That proverb stayed in my heart. It's in my heart right now, and it still comforts and inspires me. It tells me that not only do I have a path to walk, one that was set by God even before I entered this life, but I can trust God to show me how to follow that path.

Time and time again, I've found myself in situations where things were not proceeding as I'd hoped or planned, only to have God pull the curtain back and reveal that his way was so much better than any way I could have envisioned for myself. Even so, I encourage you to dare to dream. Dream big. Set your mind and heart and imagination free to envision your best possible future. Trust in the Lord with all your heart, understanding that when you don't know the way, when you're not even sure what to visualize or dream, he will show you which path to take. He may even reveal new dreams as you go along and grant you new vision as to what you can become.

And step-by-step, as you continue to walk, work, and trust, you'll move toward the fulfillment of your wildest dreams.

VISIONS FULFILLED

Do you remember those two visions I told you about—those moments in my early life when I could just *see* something that was going to happen in the future? Vision number one was that I would play pro football for the Dallas Cowboys. And vision number two was that I would play in a Super Bowl at the Rose Bowl in Pasadena. What happened to those dreams?

Well, fast-forward to the 1990 NFL draft, which I entered only after a last-second decision to turn pro even though I had one more year of eligibility at the University of Florida. After setting so many records at Florida, I was projected to go in the top ten of the 1990 NFL draft. I thought I'd probably go either to Tampa Bay— because I was a Florida native who had played for the Gators and would help bring fans to the Buccaneers games—or to Seattle, which had two picks in the top ten and needed a running back. Even though I was a huge fan of the Cowboys, Dallas was not even on my radar because their first pick was number twenty-one and I felt sure I'd be chosen by then.

On draft day I gathered with friends and family at a friend's condo on Pensacola Beach. Usually I find the beach very relaxing, but not on this occasion. As the first few picks were announced, my name was not called, and I became frustrated and nervous over my decision to leave college before my senior year. I couldn't sit still as the draft progressed. I'd hoped to go in the top ten, so I was more than a little worried when that didn't happen.

Everyone else in the condo seemed to be having a good time. I felt like the party pooper. I was worried that some faraway team would draft me and my parents would not be able to attend many games or, even worse, that I'd be selected by some team in a really cold part of the country. (I am not insulated for cold weather.)

My family and friends assured me that I'd be drafted eventually. They tried to keep my spirits up, but I was worried. Finally, during a break in the draft proceedings, I took a walk on the beach and said a little prayer: "God, it's all in your hands."

If God was running that NFL draft, he sure was making some interesting moves. The first two picks had been offensive players—first, University of Illinois quarterback Jeff George, and then a running back, Penn State's Blair Thomas. I wasn't surprised that Blair went before me because he was considered faster than me. I was glad for him.

Then the next four guys had been defensive players. Another offensive player had been chosen seventh—quarterback Andre Ware—and then eight of the next nine picks had been defensive players.

Meanwhile, I'd waited for the phone ring. It did once, around the time of the sixth pick, but it was just my brother Emory. Half of the teams in the NFL had made their picks and passed me over. It's not hard to be humble in a situation like that.

If there were any traces of cockiness left in me from my college days, they had all dried up and blown away by that point. I looked out the window, and the Gulf of Mexico was churning. So was my stomach. I had the thought that I'd better think about completing work for my degree at the University of Florida.

Then the phone rang again. The NFL draft was on its seventeenth pick. I had no idea which team owned that selection, so I was shocked when I answered the phone and my agent told me, "I've been talking to the Dallas Cowboys. Stand by."

I'd hardly hung up the phone when it rang again. It wasn't my agent this time. This caller was Cowboys coach Jimmy Johnson.

"Emmitt, how would you like to wear a star on your helmet?"

The air went out of my lungs, but I managed to tell my new coach that I would love to wear the Cowboys' star. I could not express to him what that moment meant to me. Coach Johnson had no idea that I'd been dreaming of playing for Dallas since I was a little boy watching the Cowboys on our living-room floor. I could not express to him that he hadn't selected a running back who'd bring just athletic ability to the team. They had drafted someone who was bringing his heart and soul, his dreams and his aspirations.

Because of the unusual way things worked out for me with the Dallas Cowboys, I'm convinced that God had me in his plan. I'm not alone in thinking that my selection by my dream team was the result of a very remarkable series of events. Cowboys writer Mickey Spagnola reflected on this in a column that appeared just before I was selected for the Pro Football Hall of Fame.

First, he noted that the Cowboys needed a running back from that 1990 draft because they'd previously traded Tony Dorsett and Herschel Walker. Cowboys coach Jimmy Johnson first targeted Baylor University linebacker James Francis, but Cincinnati had taken him before the Cowboys could make the move to get him. Jimmy then tried to pry James from the Bengals, but they wouldn't make a deal.

Only at that point, according to Spagnola, did the Cowboys' coaching staff decide I was their man. But then they had to swap their first-round pick with Pittsburgh and give them a third-round pick for the right to choose me as the seventeenth player taken. The fact that I ended up in Dallas after all that wheeling and dealing still makes me shake my head in wonder. The Cowboys had to go through all that to put me exactly where I'd dreamed of playing since the age of seven.

I was definitely plan B for the Cowboys in the 1990 NFL draft, but I have to think God was the ultimate player in that game. I can't pretend to understand how it all happened. But I walk in confidence that he will take me wherever he feels I need to go.

Now, hit the fast-forward button again. Six years after sharing my Super Bowl dream with my high-school buddy, I looked up into the stands from the sidelines and waved to him. It was 1993, and I was a Dallas Cowboys running back. We were playing the Buffalo Bills in Super Bowl XXVII, and we were playing at the Rose Bowl in Pasadena. It was the Cowboys' first appearance in the Super Bowl in fourteen years!

I couldn't have written a better script for those two major events in my life. I have no doubt that a higher authority orchestrated them. But both of those major accomplishments began with little more than a dream. So when I tell you to believe in the power of the human imagination, it's because so many of my visions for my life have come true.

CLAIM AND COMMIT

If you aspire to do greater things, it's up to you to claim your dreams and go after them. You can't expect greatness to come driving by so you can ask it for a ride. You have to run out in the street and grab on.

While my rookie contract was being negotiated, I had a lot of time to reflect on what I wanted to accomplish as a player in the NFL. It wasn't about the money. It was about leaving a legacy within the game. I asked myself what mark I wanted to make. That was my vision. The NFL rushing record seemed like a logical way of accomplishing that goal, although not an easy one. After all, the current record, held by the great Walter Payton, was 16,726 yards! But I decided to claim that dream—to go for it. I even did the math to figure out exactly how many yards per game I'd have to average to make the dream a reality. The answer was 125 yards per game over a thirteen-year career in the NFL. I figured if I hit that number consistently, I'd be the league's leading rusher for each season and ultimately the all-time leading rusher.

I wasn't being arrogant. I was simply taking my dream seriously—claiming it and setting up step-by-step goals that would allow me, with God's help, to achieve what I had envisioned. (We'll look at that process in more detail in a later chapter.) Now, here's an interesting thing about having the courage to claim our dreams and commit to them. Once people see that you have a vision, that you dare to dream of fulfilling it, and that you are committed to achieving your dreams, they become believers too.

So I encourage you to claim greatness. Embrace your wildest dreams and commit yourself to achieving them. Don't swagger or boast or brag, but humbly set the bar as high as you dare and commit to being the best you can possibly be. When I pursued my dreams on the football field and performed at a high level, the fans in Texas Stadium put up a sign that said "There Is No Limit to Emmitt." My teammates teased me relentlessly about that sign. Secretly, I loved what it said—not so much *about* me, but *to* other people.

That sign reflected exactly what I've been telling you: when you dare to dream and then go after your dreams with unstoppable determination, positive-minded people will line up to cheer you on. That's a lesson every man, woman, and child can benefit from. There is something highly contagious about a person who refuses to give up on a dream. How many books, movies, and stories have been created about those irrepressible dreamers? Thousands and thousands. We love those tales because the pursuit of a better life is ingrained in the human spirit.

WHEN DREAMS DON'T COME EASY

But what if dreams don't seem to come as naturally to you as they do to me? What if you don't have any grand visions? I can think of several possible reasons why that might be the case.

One may be, as I mentioned earlier, that you're simply satisfied with your life right now. There's nothing wrong with that, if you truly believe you're where you need to be. Watch out, though—because that may change. God-given visions for a new life and a new direction don't come only to little children.

It's also possible that you're just not recognizing the dreams you do have. Not everybody dreams of playing in the NFL or becoming a real-estate tycoon. Many people, for example, aspire simply to get a good job, have a happy marriage, and be good parents. All are worthy dreams—and not always easy to achieve. But because they feel ordinary or normal, you may not recognize these aspirations as dreams or visions. In this case, claiming your dream might involve simply affirming what is important to you and employing your God-given imagination to help you achieve your simple but important dreams.

But maybe there's a more serious difficulty. Maybe early in life you picked up the idea that dreams are futile and imagination is dangerous. Did anyone make fun of you for daydreaming when you were a child? Did an adult worry that you might get hurt and discourage you from reaching for something "above yourself"? Did a teacher or parent label your imagination as "lies" or come down hard on you for not being "realistic"? I'm always saddened at the ways that adults—even well-meaning adults—can step on a child's dreams. And grown-up dreams can be squelched by disapproval or failure too—to the point that you almost forget *how* to dream.

If that's true, you might need to counter this negative view of dreaming with a positive one. I hope this book will help you do that. You might even need to do a little "remedial dreaming"— take some time to get in touch with what you truly desire and what God might have in store for you.

The biggest problem I've seen with people who have trouble with dreams is that they are simply afraid to risk the unknown. Claiming your vision of a better life does take courage. It can feel like a big risk to step away from the familiar and go for something different than you have.

But that's exactly why I think you need to practice dreaming— because it makes the unfamiliar familiar. The more you go over a dream in your mind, the more your mind and heart can open up to its possibilities and make it part of you. Besides, there's no real risk in *just* dreaming, imagining what *could* be. So why not give yourself permission to start there and take the next steps when you're ready?

Ask God for the courage just to make that simple start. Just dream.

You might be surprised where he takes you from there.

DREAM IT AND DO IT

I'm an optimist by nature, and I rarely get really down about anything, but I remember a time in the seventh or eighth grade when I became discouraged about some tough homework. "I just can't do this," I said glumly.

Those were words you just didn't say with our parents around. My mother's head popped up, and she gave me an earful. "Don't ever let me hear you say you can't do something," she said. "I'm here to tell you that you can do whatever you set your heart and mind to doing. And what you can't do, God can!"

I took her words to heart, and now I'm passing them on to you. I have always done my best to serve as an example to others, particularly to those who, like me, grew up without many advantages and maybe even with some extra challenges. One of the key messages I offer to them—and now to you in this book—is that we can all rise above our circumstances. Instead of worrying about your limitations, set your heart and mind on something better.

Dreaming of the life you want will get you started and keep you motivated. Trusting in God will keep you on the right path—and I promise you he won't let you down. But you'll also have to do your part by putting yourself in position for his favor. The Bible says in James 2:26, "For as the body without the spirit is dead, so faith without works is dead also" (KJV).

I can't stress enough that you have to take responsibility for your own success. God will step in when he knows you have stepped up. A vision of greatness will take you nowhere if you fail to do the work necessary to prepare yourself. But if you do put in the sweat equity, the rewards can amaze you.

If you are willing to work hard and do whatever it takes, moving ahead one step at a time, doing as much as you can each and every day to prepare yourself for victory, you will be surprised at how the world opens up to you. I am absolutely convinced that God rewards those who are faithful, disciplined, and passionate about their visions.

I would encourage you to ask for God's help every step of the way, to ask for his guidance, and to make sure you thank him not only for any blessings that come your way, but for those you hope to receive in the future. Know that you may not have all that it takes to achieve your dreams, but God does. With his help, all things really are possible. My crazy and wonderful life is proof of that.

Yours can be too, if you start with a dream.

Believe it, and you can achieve it.

See it, and you can be it.

Dream it, and you can do it.

CHAPTER 2

PUTTING YOUR VISION INTO PLAY

Hope deferred makes the heart sick,
but a longing fulfilled is a tree of life.

PROVERBS 13:12

I HAD THINGS UNDER CONTROL, or so I thought, just before the official announcement of my selection for the Pro Football Hall of Fame class of 2010. This televised event was scheduled for Super Bowl week in Fort Lauderdale, several months before the actual induction ceremony in Canton, Ohio. I was standing backstage, reviewing my speech, when my dad appeared at my side—and dropped a bomb on me.

"Son, you know I had dreams of doing what you're doing today," he said, "but my mom got sick. So I never made it to college." Then he added softly, "You're living my dream, Son. You're living my dream."

That was *not* what I needed at that particular moment.

Being chosen for the Hall of Fame was the crowning achievement of my football career. I wanted to savor the moment with dignity in front of my family, friends, and all the fans watching on television. I had braced myself for the surge of emotions sure to come once my name was called.

But I hadn't prepared for this. Talk about opening the emotional floodgates!

Until that moment, my father had rarely offered up pieces of his past. It was even more rare for him to share the contents of his heart. I should have been focusing on my speaking points, but instead my mind went racing back to my boyhood in our Pensacola housing project and all the long hours my father put in behind the wheel of a transit bus to support our family.

Then another memory flashed, this one dating back to a visit home during my NFL career. A man about my father's age walked up to me on the street, extended his hand, and said, "Do you know who was the best running back ever to come out of Pensacola?"

At the time I was already in the NFL. I'd won a Super Bowl and all sorts of awards. So I tried to stay humble as I smiled and said, "No, who would that be?"

"Your father," said the stranger, who patted me on the back and walked away.

"Come on out here, *Emmitt Smith!*"

The sound of my name being called yanked me out of that memory and back into the present moment. My father nudged me toward the curtain and the front of the stage.

"I'm proud of you, Son," he said.

I choked up at that. All my life, I've tried to make my parents proud. And I knew they were, but that moment was really the first time my father put the *P*-word out there like that.

When I walked out on the stage, I was far from the cool, calm, and collected guy I'd hoped to be. But I did all right, or at least that's what people told me later. I threw out my prepared remarks and spoke from the heart because my father had opened his heart to me. First I shared what Pops had said backstage. Then I said that joining the Hall of Fame was an especially great honor because "I'm living his dream. I'm living my dream. And I'm fulfilling God's purpose for me."

When Pops told me his story, I felt a deeper appreciation for him and a better understanding of the choices he'd made in his life. I realized he'd never had closure over his decision not to go to college, and my success seemed to give him that closure.

I can't tell you how much it meant to me to take the name I share with my grandfather, father, and nine-year-old son, E.J., to the Pro Football Hall of Fame. It was truly a dream come true for both of us. But it took a lot more than dreaming to get us there.

A MAP FOR YOUR LIFE

In the previous chapter, I encouraged you to look beyond your circumstances and to dream big. Our dreams are the doors to lives of achievement and fulfillment. But as my father's words reminded me on that great day, dreaming isn't enough. You have to act on your dreams by going through the door and claiming the life you desire. It's one thing to dream. It's another to transform your dreams into reality so that you can fulfill the purpose God intended and follow the path he designed for you.

Think of your dreams as a football. I love the feel of a football, but it really only has value when you put it into play, right? Until then it's just an odd-shaped piece of sports equipment.

It's what you do with the football that makes it special. The same holds true for dreams. Their real value is only realized when you put them into play and then *keep* them moving. You can't score points while sitting on the sidelines. But once you start actively pursuing your dreams, you put yourself in position to make things happen.

How do you do it? The answer is simple, though doing it isn't always easy.

You put your dreams into play when you translate them into goals.

You keep those goals in front of you every day.

And then, one by one, you do your best to turn those goals into reality.

I believe I am still living my dreams because I've never stopped setting goals. In high school, college, and in my professional career, at the start of each season I'd tape my goals in my locker. Now, I tape them to the bathroom mirror at home and keep them on my desk in my office. My current goals carry some strong spiritual elements because I want to keep Jesus Christ at the head of my life, along with my family, my business, and my charities.

Goal setting is important because it helps you map out your life. It gives you a picture of where you want to go and how you hope to get there. You don't set out on a long drive without checking the map and planning how you will reach your destination. Goals work the same way. They don't guarantee success, but not setting them almost guarantees you won't get anywhere. My grandmother would put it this way: "If you fail to plan, you plan to fail."

MAKING ADJUSTMENTS

That doesn't mean that *all* your plans will succeed the way you expect. In fact, you will probably have to make some detours along the way. You may even find it impossible to get to your original destination, or you may discover a better way as you go. But the important thing is that you keep setting goals and stay behind the wheel, driving instead of being driven, moving forward instead of letting yourself get stuck in a rut.

My father's visions of his own college and professional football career were never realized, but sometimes life is more like a relay race than a simple sprint to the finish line. Dad passed on his love of sports and his athletic abilities to my brothers and me: I benefited even more from having his guidance and example. He made it possible for me to take the baton and fulfill our shared dream.

My father, whose boyhood nickname was Puddin', was a star running back at Washington High School, but he was not able to play college football or earn a degree. Fisk University's football coach offered him a scholarship, but he blew out a knee his senior year in high school. When his mother fell ill, my father had to stay home to help care for her while his own dad worked a factory job.

Talk about tough choices. But Pops stood up and did what he had to do. He and my grandfather, Emmit Sr. (known as Big Smith), are heroes to me and my brothers and sister because they lived up to their responsibilities as family men, often putting the needs of others ahead of their own desires. They were the best role models I knew while I was growing up.

My father passed on to me both his strong body and his fierce determination. I witnessed that determination many times, but especially when he decided to claim a remnant of his athletic dreams later in life. I was a senior in high school when my determined dad joined the Pensacola Wings semipro football team as a free safety. He managed to play for an entire season while still working his city-transit job.

Even back then, I thought that was amazing. But looking back now—with a better idea of what that must have required of him physically and mentally—I'm even more impressed. My father was forty-three at the time, the oldest guy on the team. But I'd hear people in the stands saying he was the best player out there. "That Puddin'," they'd say, "he's an *athlete*."

Once again he showed me, by his quiet example, that anything is possible if you are willing to dream and then do whatever it takes to make your dream come true. My father didn't play football in college or the NFL. But as my parents often told me, sometimes God's plan differs from ours.

When things didn't go as he'd dreamed, my father didn't give up. He simply adjusted and adapted. He took care of his family first, and then he joined a football team later in life. He also handed the baton to me, my brothers Erik and Emory, and my late brother, Neil, by passing on his passion for the game of football and supporting us in our efforts to excel at the sport. Believe me, I am very grateful that I had the chance to carry *our* dream into the Hall of Fame with my father still by my side.

Like my father, I've had to make adjustments in pursuing my dreams. You will too. We all have to do that sometimes, because God often surprises us with twists and turns that are beyond our capacity to foresee. Sometimes we're blindsided—on the football field and in life, too. Sometimes we uncover new information that changes our plans. Sometimes we realize we've made a mistake in our planning or that our current circumstances no longer fit our goals. Sometimes we make mistakes or simply fail and have to change course. There's nothing wrong with any of that—as long as we stay in the game.

Life can be unpredictable. So the best you and I can do is to make our plans and then expect the unexpected. We must be flexible, adapt to changes and challenges, and trust that God will guide us. We may be lucky enough to achieve some or even all of our dreams, or we may have the privilege of passing the baton on to someone who shares them. But neither is likely to happen unless we get serious about translating our dreams into solid, specific goals.

A LESSON IN GOAL SETTING

I had some sense of that as I was growing up, but my high school coach Dwight Thomas really drove the point home for me. He talked often about setting goals and working to meet them, and he also walked the walk. He is such an inspirational man. My emotional connection to him is so strong it's just crazy, and it's difficult to express just how much the man has meant to me.

Coach Thomas was the defensive coordinator for the Merritt Island (Florida) High School football team when they won the state championship in 1972. Then, just before coming to Pensacola, he'd been head coach at Choctawhatchee High School in Fort Walton Beach, forty miles to the east. His Fort Walton team won thirty games and lost only twelve in his first four years there.

Going into his fifth year, the 1983 season, Coach Thomas had fifteen seniors returning. Many people felt another state championship was a real possibility for his team. Then, just before that season started, the principal of the school asked for his resignation. The principal said the school was positioned to win a state championship, but for some reason he didn't think Coach Thomas could make it happen. He asked for Coach Thomas's formal resignation by four thirty that day.

That was a tough blow, but Coach Thomas is a tough guy. He quit one minute before the deadline and told the principal, "I'm going to find the worst team in the state and come back here and kick your butt." (I'm sure he used a different word to make the point!)

Coach used his hurt and anger as motivation. He decided then and there that he would find another team to take to the top, and he planned on beating the Fort Walton team on the way there. Dwight Thomas had the vision, he set a goal, and then he turned it into a reality, despite some very tough challenges. You see, his next job was coaching my school, Pensacola's Escambia High School, where the football team could claim only one winning season in the previous eighteen years.

The year before Coach Thomas arrived, the team had lost every game. He had to set new standards, and he did. He insisted on discipline on the practice field and in the classroom, and when his rules were not followed, he cleaned house. At the start of his first year, my freshman year, there were thirty-eight seniors on the team. By the first game, there were only seven of those seniors left because the others had broken his orders not to skip school.

I was a freshman that year—Coach Thomas's first. He had never allowed a freshman to be a starter on the varsity team. But he chose to start two of us that year, along with eleven sophomores. I ran for 1,525 yards and 19 touchdowns. My sophomore year, I rushed for 2,424 yards and 26 touchdowns. We won our first 3A state football championship in the school's history after I ran for 198 yards in the final game. The next season, my junior year, we were bumped up to the 4A division. I rushed for 2,918 yards and 33 touchdowns, and again we won the state championship in our division.

We had some very good players, but we had an even better coach, who taught us as much about life as he did about football. One day during my sophomore year, Coach Thomas handed out five-by-ten-inch index cards to each of us. He said it was fine to have dreams and to share them with others, "But it's only a dream until you write it down," he said. "Then it becomes a goal."

Coach Thomas challenged each of us not only to write down goals that would carry us to achieve our dreams, but to get specific about *how* we planned to achieve those goals. When I told him I wanted to break the Florida high-school record for rushing, he pulled out the Florida High School Athletic Association record book, and I looked up how many yards that would take. Coach Thomas taught me to do that for my other goals as well—to take them seriously enough to do the math and make a plan.

All through my athletic career, a lot of people—sportswriters, coaches, other players, scouts, and fans—have claimed I wasn't that fast or that strong or that great a runner. I never argued with them. I just went out and did the best I could. And maybe the critics were correct. There probably have been many faster and stronger running backs than me.

So what set me apart? I think it was the lesson I learned from Coach Thomas. Even though I crossed the goal line many times as a running back, my biggest claim to fame may be that I wasn't just a goal scorer. I was also a goal *keeper*.

I was continually in the process of taking my dreams, turning them into goals, making and revising my strategy to achieve them, and then chasing after them as fast as my feet could fly. No matter what happened in my life, my goal keeping kept my dreams in constant play.

THE POWER OF GOAL KEEPING

Early in my rookie season with the Dallas Cowboys, I met with owner Jerry Jones, who'd made a lot of money in the oil and gas exploration business before buying the team. I gave Jerry my list of goals—my business goals as well as those pertaining to football—and I asked him to check those he thought he could help me achieve.

He read the list and then checked every one of my goals. "We'll get to some of these now and some of these later," he said, "but we'll get to all of them sooner or later."

My goals for my rookie year with the Cowboys did not lack for ambition. I told Jerry Jones my plan was to win a Super Bowl, be named Offensive Rookie of the Year for the NFL, and to make the Pro Bowl. Despite my plan, the Cowboys didn't make the Super Bowl that year. But our 7–9 season was a vast improvement over the previous season's 1–15, and that turnaround won Jimmy Johnson NFL Coach of the Year. I did manage to be named the NFL Offensive Rookie of the Year, and I made my first Pro Bowl—not a bad start as far as achieving my season's goals.

We came on strong the next two seasons. In the 1991 season, I won my first NFL rushing title with 1,563 yards—the youngest player, at age twenty-two, to win a season-rushing crown. In the 1992 season I set a Cowboys rushing record and won another NFL rushing title with 1,713 yards. Even better, my team won the Super Bowl!

By then there were plenty of accolades coming my way, but I sensed I was just getting started. I woke up one morning just before the 1993 season feeling very goal oriented, so I wrote out a whole new list. I decided to make these goals both specific and ambitious:

- Keep Jesus Christ number one in my life.
- Stay healthy.
- Average 125 yards rushing per game.
- Lead the team and league in rushing for the third year in a row.
- Lead the league in scoring.
- Rush for more than 1,000 yards by the eighth game.
- Catch seventy passes.
- Do not fumble—ever!
- Go to the Pro Bowl for my fourth year.
- Be named to the first team of the NFL All-Pro Team.
- Be named MVP of the NFL.
- Go to the Super Bowl and win again.
- Earn the Super Bowl MVP award.
- Go to Disneyland.

Quite a list for a young guy, don't you think? I discussed those goals recently with a friend who said they reflected an "audacious vision." It didn't seem that audacious to me, though. My feeling at the time was that I had proved myself in high school and college and had already achieved many of my previous goals, so I wanted to build on that success in the NFL and beyond. I didn't have doubts. I had dreams fueled by visions of accomplishment, and I knew from experience that setting goals and striving toward them was the only way to move toward those dreams.

I also had learned by that point that past victories are stepping-stones to future achievements. Looking at what I had already accomplished gave me confidence that I could build on that past success. That's one piece of advice I would give regarding goal keeping. When you set your goals, think of goals you've already achieved, and build on those strengths if you can.

I ended that 1993 season more convinced than ever of the power of turning my dreams into goals and my goals into reality. Looking back, it almost seems crazy. But in that great year I became the only running back ever to win a Super Bowl championship, earn the NFL rushing crown, be named NFL Player of the Year and Super Bowl MVP, and be honored with the Bert Bell Professional Player of the Year award. Those accomplishments seem even crazier when you consider that I sat out the first two games of the season because Jerry Jones and I were tussling over my new contract. I went to Disneyland that year too.

There was one goal I did not achieve in 1993, however. I did not lead the league in scoring. Oakland Raiders kicker Jeff Jaeger took that title. In fact, kickers won the scoring title every year in the entire decade of the 1990s—except for one. That was 1995, when I finally made that elusive goal.

A NEW DREAM, A NEW GOAL

Based on the success of my efforts as a goal keeper, I kept setting the bar higher and higher, wanting to push my talents as far as they would take me. Then, just before the 1996 season, I had a series of very intense and realistic dreams about my longtime hero and role model, Walter Payton. (I've never stopped dreaming, even while I'm working to make my dreams into goals and my goals into reality.) I'd see him running the "rock" in uniform against various opponents—making a move, cutting through a gap, or pushing through a pileup of Vikings or Lions or Patriots.

I usually dream in Technicolor, just like the movies. Now it was like watching my own personal Walter Payton highlight reel.

What did the dreams mean? I believed they were telling me that I should keep pursing my goal of leading the NFL in career rushing with even more focus.

The previous season had been the best of my career for yards rushing. I'd had 1,773 yards on the ground in 1995, which put me at 8,956 total yards for my NFL career so far. (I'd run nearly the same total yards in my four years in high school.) I was doing very well as an NFL running back. But now I wondered what it would take to be the leading rusher of all time in the league. To do that, I'd have to beat Walter Payton's record.

When I was a boy running around the park, I'd often envision myself as Walter, running in a Chicago Bears uniform with the number 34 and a big *C* on the helmet. In high school, I had the man's picture taped to my football locker and his nickname, "Sweetness," stitched onto my letterman's jacket. When some of the girls in my high school started calling me "Sweetness," I did not discourage them, not at all.

I especially loved Payton's running style. He could be elusive, but he could run right over people too. And he got results. Walter Payton had rushed for nearly 17,000 yards over the course of his NFL career. Could I do better than that?

It wasn't that I wanted to "beat" my hero. Walter was my role model, so I set my sights on doing what he did and maybe a little more. My recurring visions of Payton on the football field seemed like a powerful sign that this was part of God's plan too. But beating Payton's record was no small goal. In fact, at that point in my career, it was downright scary to consider what I'd need to do to catch and surpass one of the greatest running backs to play the game.

Following Coach Thomas's advice, I pulled out a piece of paper and wrote down Walter's record-breaking yardage. Then, below it, I wrote "9,000 yards," which was about my total yardage for the Cowboys up to that point.

I did the math, and the result left me wondering if I'd lost my mind. How would I ever gain enough yards to break Walter's record? Would my body hold up another seven or eight years? I was already reaching the point where I didn't bounce back quickly from all the punishment I took on the field. Sure, I had won a number of rushing titles and Super Bowls and many accolades, but did I have the stamina to keep it up year after year? All of those things danced around in my mind, but I tried to stay humble and hungry as I considered what it would take to reach my goal of surpassing Walter Payton's rushing record.

This called for some more serious scrambling. Walter had played until the age of thirty-three. I was twenty-six years old. I figured that even if I gained 1,500 yards a season for the next five years, I'd still come up short by a couple hundred yards, because Walter's actual career yardage was 16,726.

I did have youth on my side. I figured that in five years, I'd be thirty-one—two years younger than Walter had been when he retired.

As it turned out, my math was a little off. What I did not calculate was the effect that losing my teammates would have on me. Daryl "Moose" Johnston and Troy Aikman and Charlie Haley retired over the next five years—Michael Irvin, too. Not having my Super Bowl teammates was like losing pieces of myself. They were my friends and teammates, all winners. And readjusting to new teammates slowed me down a little. So I needed an extra year to catch Walter and achieve my goal—but I did get there.

On Sunday, October 27, 2002, the Cowboys were playing the Seattle Seahawks at Texas Stadium. At the start of the game, I was only 93 yards short of Walter Payton's all-time record.

I woke up that morning with the confidence that this would be the day. We had the home crowd, and it was important to me that this record be celebrated by the Texas fans who had supported me so long. This was not a day to fail, I told myself. I was not coming up short. It would be a great day. That was my mind-set.

Other people were thinking that way too. Jerry Jones already had ordered up a big banner and a celebration. Before the game, my teammate Reggie Swinton came over and told me, "I want to be the first one to congratulate you on breaking this record. I know it will be crazy after this game, but I want you to know now that it's an honor to play with you."

So now all I had to do was get out there and break that record—no pressure or anything. No one had to remind me that I hadn't run for a hundred yards in a game so far that season. Still, I was determined not to disappoint the owner or the fans. I was going to run for more than one goal that day.

I'm not much for creating drama, but I managed to keep the suspense up during that game. With ten minutes left on the clock, I was still thirteen yards short of Walter's record. Every time I got the ball, the crowd rose in anticipation. They were going crazy, and I loved their enthusiasm and support. But if the game ended without my achieving this goal, I knew I'd face a long week of questions from the media, fans, my parents, brothers, sister, friends, and probably my wife and kids.

I did my best to keep focused on the game, but it would be a fib to say the record wasn't on my mind as I played. Before the game, I had another vision of Walter Payton running with me down the field. Everything slowed down in the movie that played out in my mind. I thought of Walter Payton with respect and gratitude. I sent off a mental thank-you note to him.

He'd given me vision that grew into a dream.

Then it became a goal.

Now it was about to become a reality.

I tracked every yard as I ran. I was grinding them out bit by bit.

I gained three yards on a first-down handoff. Then in the huddle our quarterback, Chad Hutchinson, called another handoff to me. I sprinted off left tackle. There wasn't much of a hole, but I pushed through the line, cut to the left, and found some room to run.

Someone hit me, but I managed to bounce off. And thanks to a massive block from our fullback, Robert Thomas, I picked up a couple more yards. Then I was tripped up a little when I stumbled over another Cowboy who had fallen in my path. But before I went down all the way I put an arm on the ground and pushed myself forward for another yard or two—the yard or two I needed.

The stadium exploded with blinding flashes from thousands of cameras as fans and media photographers captured the moment. Fireworks went off. I'd never seen that while a game was still in progress. I looked up and thanked God, and then I thanked Walter Payton.

I took off my Cowboys helmet, basking in the moment. Vision fulfilled. Dream done. Goal accomplished. I knelt near the thirty-yard line and thanked God and Walter again.

This was a first-time experience for me, so I really didn't know what to do next. One of the refs called me to the sideline, where he handed me the game ball and said, "Congratulations." Then I started to run back to the field, thinking they might throw a flag on me for delaying the game. My laughing teammates motioned toward the sidelines, where my family stood waiting for me.

Apparently the game was in time-out, and the show was on.

I walked over to my mother and father, who were practically dancing with joy. My wife, Pat, and the kids stood behind Mom and Pops, and I hugged them. Then I spotted my retired teammates

Michael Irvin and Moose Johnston, the human wrecking ball who had cleared the way for me so many times. I didn't lose it until I hugged the man who had sacrificed so much of his career and life to help the Cowboys win and to help me achieve my personal goals.

After five or ten minutes of crazy celebration, we went back to finish the football game. The quarterback handed me the football, and I realized that even though I'd accomplished my goal, I still needed to keep running. In fact, I scored on a one-yard run that tied the game 14–14. Unfortunately, the Seahawks kicked a last-minute field goal, and we lost the game.

I thought that might dampen the fans' enthusiasm, but I was wrong. There were nearly sixty-four thousand of them in the stands, and none of them wanted to leave after the game was over. I exited the field with my teammates after the game, but the cheering continued, so I went back out to thank the fans as the new NFL all-time rushing leader.

PRINCIPLES OF GOAL KEEPING

Every time that moment comes to mind, one of the thoughts that strikes me is that without Coach Thomas and his wisdom, I might never have taken that dream and made it a reality. His method for transforming dreams into reality through goal keeping really works. When you write down your goals, work out a plan, and then keep your goals in mind every day, you breathe life into them. There's something about the process that pulls dreams out of the realm of possibility and into the real world.

But should every dream become a goal? Probably not. It's a

good idea to consider whether a particular dream is silly, crazy, unethical, or unachievable. You have to ground your goals in common sense and your sense of God's purpose for your life.

At the same time, don't be afraid to set goals so lofty that you'll have to grow to accomplish them. Here are a few principles to keep in mind as you work to translate your dreams into goals and your goals into your reality.

Goal-Keeping Principle #1: Keep Focused

Feel free to dream as big as your imagination will allow, but when turning those dreams into goals, you need to bring them into focus. Consider what you truly want for your life in both the short term and the long term, and set your goals accordingly. Then, once you've spelled them out and written them down, those goals will help keep you focused on what you need to do to achieve your dreams.

When I was writing out my goals for Coach Thomas, for example, I realized my dreams weren't just about football. I did want to play in college and the NFL. But I also wanted to become a successful businessman. I wanted to help my family and, later, to have a family of my own and build a legacy for future generations.

Those long-term goals helped focus my short-term goals. For example, I wanted to do well in football, but I also needed to keep my grades up to be eligible for a scholarship to a good college or university. Playing college ball at the University of Florida was a thrill, and I made great friends in Gainesville, but it, too, was a short-term goal—a stepping-stone to my long-term goal of signing a professional football contract and completing my education so I'd be prepared for life after football.

Even while playing for the Dallas Cowboys, I kept in mind my long-term goal of being a businessman. So I took every opportunity to meet with and talk to the businesspeople I encountered during those years, and I looked for former athletes who had successful business careers.

We may be lucky enough to achieve some or even all of our dreams, or we may have the privilege of passing the baton on to someone who shares them. But neither is likely to happen unless we get serious about translating our dreams into solid, specific goals.

One of the best in both arenas was former Cowboys quarterback Roger Staubach, who sold his very successful real-estate brokerage firm in 2010 for more than $600 million. Another was NBA star Michael Jordan, whose business empire includes shoe and clothing lines, motorcycle racing, restaurants, and majority ownership of the Charlotte Bobcats, not to mention legendary endorsement deals. Another NBA star, Dave Bing, became a respected entrepreneur and businessman and then mayor of Detroit. And NBA legend Earvin "Magic" Johnson has made a very successful transition into the business world with a variety of enterprises, including coffee and fast-food franchises, fitness centers, and food-service companies as well as real-estate development. All these became role models for me as I considered what it would take to achieve my long-term business goals. Throughout my life and career, writing down my short- and long-term goals and always keeping them close by has helped me stayed focused and on track. It's not necessary and not even possible to always have your goals at the forefront of your mind. Life happens, and sometimes it seems to come at you at 150 miles per hour. But when you write down your goals and put them where you can read them at least once a day, you can check your progress toward them on a regular basis and keep yourself focused on where you're going.

Nearly every day, in some way big or small, I try to take actions that move me closer to achieving the goals I have written down. I also try to sit down regularly to reassess my goals. When I was still playing football, games and practices kept me pretty busy during the season, but the off-seasons gave me time to change my plans if necessary. My football career worked out almost exactly as I'd hoped, but I did have to make some adjustments along the way, as we all must do.

I had intended to play four years at the University of Florida, for example, because I'd promised my mother I would earn a degree. But a series of coaching changes at the university and the opportunity for a life-changing NFL contract caused me to reconsider. I left school for the pros after my junior year. But I went back and finished my degree later to keep my promise to myself and to my mother.

You may need to make adjustments on your journey to your goals too. The important thing is that even when circumstances force you to change your short-term goals, staying focused on your long-term goals will help you adjust and keep going.

Goal-Keeping Principle #2: Center Your Goals on Your Values

Priorities change over the course of a lifetime. My father's priorities changed. Mine have changed. Yours will change too. What may seem like a wonderful long-term goal when you are twenty-five may no longer be desirable when you are forty-five. Even so, your goals must be centered on your core beliefs and values.

My goals, for example, are based on my Christian beliefs and values. I want to honor God in all that I do and obey him. Everything I hope to do involves creating a secure and happy life for my family while using every gift God has given me. That means I would never knowingly set a goal that might endanger the welfare of my family, squander my gifts and talents, or exploit people in some way. I try to set goals that help me be the best possible person I can be—and to me, that means someone with loving and lasting relationships and a strong spiritual foundation.

Being inducted into the Hall of Fame was a tremendous honor. That day was the realization of a dream that became a goal that became a reality. But as I said in my speech during the announcement ceremony, what I value most about my playing days is the bonds formed with my teammates, coaches, fans, and others involved in the game. That's one reason I became so emotional during my speech that day. It wasn't the award itself I received. It was the honor I felt to have the respect and friendship of all those gathered for the ceremony and watching on television.

My goals are centered first on my relationship with God and then on my relationships with family and friends. I see those relationships as the most important and most valuable assets in my life. Now, I do have some other assets here and there, and I'm grateful for them. But if they were to disappear tomorrow, I'd be okay because my sense of self is not wrapped up in what I own. I enjoy material things, but they are not what I truly value.

For example, my achievements in football and business have

allowed me to have a very nice house, one that is much larger than the house I grew up in. But do you know what I really value most about our home in Dallas? Every day I'm grateful that the rooms in our house are filled with every bit as much love and caring as the much smaller house I grew up in back in Pensacola. The house my father built in my grandparents' backyard didn't have nearly as much square footage. But its capacity for love was as big as any mansion I've ever seen—and it's the love that matters most.

When you make your goals God centered, you focus not on what you want for yourself, but on what God wants to do *through* you. That probably doesn't mean you can just sit around and wait for God to spell out exactly what he wants you to do. As far as I can tell, that's not the way things usually work. Instead, you read the Bible, seek wise counsel, pray, and get a good sense of what matters to God. Then you look at your dreams and the gifts you've been given, take an inventory, and set goals that allow you to develop and use your gifts to their highest purpose. And remember, you can always adjust your goals later if you sense God has something new in mind.

Set your goals with the understanding that God will make his plan for you known in his own way on his own schedule. Center those goals on the values and principles that will serve you for a lifetime. To me, that's the key to real satisfaction.

Goal-Keeping Principle #3: Consider Your Heritage and Your Legacy

Our job on this earth, as I see it, is not complicated. We must strive to do our best, make the most of our gifts, and as much as possible, leave the world a better place. I know that may sound a little naive, but I believe you have to aim high. To accomplish that mission, I set goals that are focused, centered on my values and principles, and also rooted in the belief that each of us is a part of something bigger than ourselves.

Sometimes people lose sight of the fact that we are all links in a vast network, connected to those who came before us and those who will follow. As different as we may think we are, the truth is that we are all branches of the same tree of humanity. Black, white, Asian, Hispanic, whatever, we all sprang from the same roots. The goals that we choose to guide us must acknowledge that common humanity, that connectedness, and our duty both to honor our past and build upon it for the future. We do that by remembering our heritage, expressing gratitude for it, and doing our part in our allotted time to prepare the way and smooth the path for those who come after us.

I'd always thought I had a powerful sense of purpose and a great appreciation for the gift of my life, but in the summer of 2009 I came to value this much, much more. The depth of my appreciation increased when I took a trip back in time and traced my roots. I discovered that the more I knew about my ancestry, the more I wanted to build on my forefathers' legacy and make my own contribution.

It all began when I filmed a pilot episode for a television reality show called *Who Do You Think You Are?*, produced by former *Friends* star Lisa Kudrow. My experiences doing that show made me look more deeply than ever before into who I am and what my purpose is on this planet.

Who Do You Think You Are? was adapted from a British

television series and offers history lessons while tracing the ancestry of celebrity guest stars. The show features experts who are skilled at digging into old public documents—tax rolls, property deeds, and census reports as well as birth, marriage, and death records. These experts take the guest star and a film crew along on their investigation, tracing back through the generations to identify ancestors and their legacies.

The search for my roots with the crew from *Who Do You Think You Are?* took me first from Pensacola, Florida, where I grew up, to Burnt Corn, Alabama, where my father's mother's family lived, and then on to Mecklenburg County, Virginia, where my ancestors were owned as plantation slaves. Then our journey took us even farther, beyond the United States to West Africa.

Taping the show was a wild ride. I hadn't anticipated it would be such an emotional experience. Like most people, I knew only bits and pieces of my family's history. I had often wondered why I was considered an African American instead of simply an American. During the show's taping, I came to understand that I am a true African American.

The researchers confirmed that my grandmother's father, Frank Watson, an entrepreneur and landowner, was the son of Bill and Victoria Watson. Bill was born into slavery, like most blacks of his generation, but after the Emancipation Proclamation freed the slaves, he lived as a free man in Burnt Corn, Alabama, about a hundred miles south of Birmingham.

I'd always been told that I had some Native American ancestry on my grandmother's side, and it turned out that Burnt Corn sits at what was once a trading crossroads of the Muscogee (Creek)

Nation. A DNA test confirmed our family story, revealing that my genetic makeup is roughly 7 percent Native American. Thanks to the show's researchers, I learned that one of my slave ancestors was the offspring of a slave mother and, in all likelihood, a white slave-owner father. This, too, was confirmed by my DNA report, which found that my genes were about 12 percent European.

The analysis also noted that my DNA is roughly 81 percent African, which is considered high for an African American. In fact, the analysis qualified me as "quintessentially African." I like that! The show's team of genealogy experts determined from my DNA that my African ancestors likely came from what is now the Republic of Benin, in a part of West Africa known as the Slave Coast because of the slave trade that once thrived there.

This was all amazing information, though I found some of it disturbing. My slave ancestor Mariah Puryear, for example, was most likely impregnated by her white owner and then turned over to his son along with a bridle and saddle, according to documents uncovered by the show's investigators. Seeing the names of Mariah and her children listed as "property" in a public document brought home the reality of slavery like never before. There it was on paper—that my own ancestors had been bought and sold like livestock. I kept thinking about what their lives must have been like, what they'd had to endure just to survive, and how I owed my existence to their determination and perseverance.

Because of the incredible life God has provided for me, I believe in destiny. Even so, I was more than a little stunned when our research into Mariah Puryear led us to the actual record of her sale in 1826 in Mecklenburg County, Virginia. We found that record in the county's Deed Book 22—the same number I'd worn on my jersey through most of my college and professional career. Quite the coincidence, wouldn't you say?

Still, the most stunning part of this investigation into my roots was the connection I felt when the show's producers took me to visit my ancestral home in West Africa. We visited a history museum in a former fort that had housed slaves and their jailers. After separating the weak from the strong, the jailers marched those judged fit for the journey onto the boats. We saw the port from which kidnapped and shackled Africans were shipped across the Atlantic Ocean.

I walked on the Benin beach looking out over the Atlantic Ocean, thousands of miles and light-years away from the comforts of my own life, and the thought struck me: *I'm only here because my ancestors survived that crossing. I am here because they overcame the challenges of slavery, racism, poverty, and cruelties that I can only imagine.*

My emotions ran high during that visit to my African homeland, just as they had when the show took me to the towns in Virginia and Alabama where my black, white, and Native American ancestors had lived. Some were heroes; I have no doubt. Some were villains—I'm sure of that, too. Still, I am connected to them all, and I can only aspire to embrace the good in all of them while striving to build upon the best.

While taping our episode, it hit me that none of us walks this earth alone. We walk with God, and we stand on the shoulders of giants who came before us. Since that show, whatever goals I set have been chosen, at least in part, to honor the memory of those who came before me, especially those who suffered and struggled to endure. My life is the product of their struggles. My goals are rooted in their journey.

You, too, are the product of all who came before you. Their struggles and striving helped make your life possible. Our accomplishments are built upon the hard work and striving of our parents, grandparents, great-grandparents, and all who came before us. I encourage you to set goals that honor that contribution and advance the dreams of your children, grandchildren, great-grandchildren, and all who descend from your family tree.

But this principle doesn't apply only to family. So many people in past generations have contributed to your present life. So many people can benefit from your choices. When you transform your dreams into goals and your goals into reality, know that you are continuing a journey begun by those who preceded you. Remember also that those who follow you will build upon your accomplishments and achievements.

Someone asked me recently how I managed to stay on track and, for the most part, make good decisions throughout my life, so far. I've thought about that a lot, and I believe I have an answer. I'm no saint by any stretch of the imagination, and I certainly have my limitations. But I've chosen to learn a lot from my failures and mistakes. And more important, I've been determined not to let my family down. Now that I also have a fan base, I'm responsible to them, too. Isn't it funny that I feel responsible to people I don't even know!

After tracing my roots, I feel even more committed to honoring my parents, especially, but all of my ancestors. My experiences filming the show reminded me of just how many others struggled and sacrificed so that I might be able to enjoy the life I have. When your goals have roots like that, the motivation to build a legacy is powerful.

Goal-Keeping Principle #4: Hold On to Your Passion and Your Purpose

My dreams often inspire my goals, but before I write them down and put them into action, I make sure each goal is based on purpose—my purpose on this planet as chosen by my heavenly Father. Sometimes I hear people saying they haven't found their purpose. If that's the case with you, I'd suggest that maybe you are looking in the wrong place. You won't discover your true purpose in a college classroom, at a job fair, or through the help-wanted ads. In fact, I don't think you can actually "choose your purpose." More accurately, your purpose chooses you. It's already within your heart. Your job is to find it.

Your purpose springs from your passion—whatever it is you do that gives you so much pleasure and fulfillment that you find yourself drawn to do it whenever and wherever possible. For many, a passion is obvious from an early age. Think of the child who can't be torn away from the piano or the garden or the fishing boat or the drawing pad. Childhood passions are like childhood dreams. They are God's hints about the path or purpose he has planned for you.

Don't let anyone else dictate to you or force you to follow a path he or she has chosen. You will never be truly fulfilled unless you follow the path paved by your God-given passion. Instead of being concerned about living up to the expectations of others, focus on setting high expectations for yourself. Take responsibility for your own happiness and fulfillment. Tell your own story based on what God has written in your heart. Let your passion drive your purpose, because if you love what you do, you will always be able to find the commitment necessary to sacrifice and persevere.

But can passion become a problem? The Bible, after all, warns about being "enslaved by all kinds of passions and pleasures" (Titus 3:3). But that's not what I'm talking about at all. The trouble is that the word *passion* has several different meanings. It can refer to a fleeting emotion or desire or even a selfish compulsion. But it also indicates an intense attraction or interest, and that's what I mean here. Your passion is the internal energy that can lead you to your purpose. And your purpose goes beyond yourself. This is the path you are meant to follow, your destiny, and the mark you were meant to make on this earth.

That's not to say you have only one passion and only one purpose. In fact, you might have quite a few over the course of a lifetime, though some will be more important than others. I had a passion for football, but it wasn't my only passion. And my purpose wasn't simply to be a good football player. If that was the case, I should have retired to a small island as soon as my NFL career ended. How much fun would that be?

When I fulfilled my dream as a football player and entered the Hall of Fame, I was following that passion and pursuing a couple of purposes. As I mentioned earlier, I was helping my father realize his dream through me, and I was using the talents and gifts God had planted within me to give him glory and also to position myself for even higher achievements.

I credit God for blessing me with a long and fulfilling football career. But I don't think he's done with me yet. As long as you and I are still living and breathing, we have a purpose to serve. Maybe your purpose is to accomplish great things, or maybe it is to inspire others to great accomplishments. Just know that if you are here, there is a reason. So I would encourage you to always keep setting goals and figuring out how to achieve them.

I noted in the previous chapter that my many hours in that Pensacola park also included long sessions in which my brothers, our friends, and I mapped out entire neighborhoods on our dirt drawing boards. That childhood pastime was a clue to another passion within me, a desire to develop and build things that would enhance the quality of life for others while allowing me to leave a legacy for my own family.

When I was eight to eleven years old, playing Pop Warner football in Pensacola, I'd sometimes spend the night before games at the home of my coach, Charlie Edgar, who had boys of his own. The Edgars had a home that appeared to be about 3,500 square feet, much bigger than our place in the projects. I asked him how he'd come to own such a nice house.

"I built it myself," he said.

Coach Edgar's family had a small construction company. After talking with him, I became interested in building and architecture. I liked the idea of building something of value where there hadn't been anything before. So I asked Coach Edgar a lot of questions about his business and how it worked. One of the first things he showed me was a construction blueprint for one of his building projects. The blueprint took a design or a dream and made it a reality by mapping out the construction process step-by-step.

As he talked about his construction business, I realized the passion my coach had for his trade was just as strong as his passion for football. He opened up my eyes to the fact that you could build your life around the things you love to do. I was so inspired by Coach Edgar that I initially wanted to major in architecture in college, but my guidance counselors told me that would be too demanding a major for someone who was a starter on the college team. Still, my interest in construction and real estate stayed with me over the years, and when I could no longer perform to my own highest expectations in sports, I moved on without looking back.

Well, that's not exactly true. I had been looking back for quite a while, back to Coach Edgar and his blueprints, back even to those neighborhoods etched in the dirt. I didn't want to be one of those athletes who are unprepared for life after sports, so I'd been doing my homework.

After my rookie season with the Cowboys, I began buying and selling real estate in Dallas and back in Pensacola. I continued doing that in the off-seasons throughout my football career. I also asked Roger Staubach to help me learn more about the commercial real-estate business. In 2005, Roger and I launched a joint venture called SmithCypress Partners.

Then after a couple of years the market turned, and I joined with some others to create ESmith Legacy, a minority-owned real-estate-development business based in Dallas, with offices in Baltimore and Philadelphia. ESmith Legacy specializes in finding undervalued properties with high potential in urban areas and developing them. Our projects include Zenith, a retail and condo building in Baltimore with 191 luxury units and 6,000 square feet of retail space; another Baltimore project at 414 Water Street, which is a thirty-one-story luxury condominium complex in Baltimore with views of the city's Inner Harbor; and our Harlem project at 125th Street and Lenox Avenue.

The name of the company reflects my long-term goal of leaving a legacy for my children and grandchildren and also for generations to come. I had a wonderful football career, but this new career allows me to build something lasting in bricks and mortar that will benefit people long after I'm gone.

God blessed me with a great football career. I believe he will do the same in my business career because he knows my passion for the real-estate and building business. God put that passion in my heart. If that wasn't where he wanted me, he would not have put that vision there. I am 100 percent convinced that this is my purpose.

So what's your passion and purpose? If you haven't identified it yet, maybe you haven't paid attention to the clues God has sent your way. What is it that you are always drawn to? What do your parents, teachers, and friends compliment you on and encourage you to do? What always intrigues you? Why?

Take a few minutes, and think about what clues you might have missed. They shouldn't be that hard to identify. Call to mind those times in your life when you've found yourself engaged in an activity that you enjoyed and found so stimulating that you lost track of time and place, something that seemed to mesh with all your interests and abilities. That will give you a clue about your passions and maybe even your purpose.

We must use our God-given gifts and passions to make the world a better place, whether in big ways or small. Your long-term goals must always be to pursue your passions and to fulfill your purpose by leaving a legacy that has a positive impact and that somehow, in some way, helps and inspires others to bring their dreams into reality.

CHAPTER 3

FOLLOW YOUR PATH

Endurance develops strength of character,
and character strengthens our confident hope of salvation.

ROMANS 5:4, NLT

IT'S A STORY THAT'S been repeated many times before. But when I heard it for the first time, it seemed to be drawn from my own life, so I want to retell it here in my own words. It's the story of a regular man of faith who one night had a powerful dream.

In the dream, the man was walking with God, side-by-side, on a beautiful beach just like those in Pensacola where I grew up. But the sky was lit up like one giant movie screen, even bigger than the six-hundred-ton JumboTron in the Dallas Cowboys' new stadium. As the man of faith walked with the Lord, they watched major events in his life captured in the bright sky like scenes in a video.

After each happy scene capturing his birthdays, graduation, marriage, the birth of his children, holiday gatherings, and other great moments, another slide would appear showing two sets of footprints tracing a path in the sand. One set belonged to the man. The other belonged to God. But after each sad scene in which he'd experienced failure or heartbreak, the next slide would show only one set of footprints in the sand.

This part of the dream really bothered the man, so at one point he asked, "Lord, when I promised to always have faith, I thought you would walk with me in good times and in bad. But from what I'm seeing now, it looks like you weren't there when I needed you the most."

God smiled at the man like a father upon his child.

"My son," the Lord said, "when you saw just one set of footprints in the sand, it was because I was carrying you through those challenging times."

After hearing that powerful story in church one day, I told my wife that I knew exactly when I was walking on my own and when God was carrying me. At every turning point, the Lord lifted me up and carried me through. He is always with us. That's why I walk in confidence today, knowing that my Lord and Savior has prepared me to do great things and that what I lack, he will provide.

The same is true for you. God prepares us for the paths he has chosen for us. Sometimes, it just takes us a while to find that path. Some never find it because they give up. Others find the way but struggle to stay on course. That is why it is so important to sense God's footprints with you along the way. In many ways the steps you choose to follow will shape the person you're going to be. Your path and your character just can't be separated.

THE CONTENT OF OUR CHARACTER

God prepared me for my walk on this earth by giving me, first of all, the gift of faith—a gift that I've always acknowledged but have come to appreciate fully only in recent years. Then the Lord granted me the power to dream beyond my circumstances, and he guided me to set goals that moved me along his path.

Yes, I've fallen off the path from time to time. We all do. But I've always managed to find my way back because God also provided guides who have instilled in me the beliefs and principles that serve as my markers. He's provided them to you as well. The extent to which we choose to follow these principles and act on these beliefs determines what Rev. Martin Luther King Jr. called "the content of [our] character."

How high you go in life and what kind of legacy you leave behind relate directly to the depth and strength of your character. I spent enough time around my grandparents and other older folks to see that as you reach the end of your life, what you've acquired and what you've done aren't nearly as important as who you are and what you represent to those around you. The Bible tells us this too, promising that "endurance develops strength of character, and character strengthens our confident hope of salvation" (Romans 5:4, NLT).

Character development is an inside-out process. The quality of what lies inside you determines the quality of your life in the outside world. If you aspire to be a leader of great impact, then you must first develop the depth of character required for such a role. If you want to be respected by your loved ones and your peers, then you have to develop a character worthy of their respect.

A MATTER OF PRINCIPLE

Principles are age-old, natural laws proven time and again over many years. I've heard it said that you can't break them, but you can break yourself against them. They are present in the teachings of every religion, but they aren't religious concepts by nature. They are also the basis of many criminal and civil laws, but they aren't laws in themselves. The generally accepted principles of society spring from our humanity, and they are probably a major reason the human race has endured. The core principles must be followed if we are to live, work, and play together in harmony.

Honesty, for example, is a principle that most people value. If most of us weren't honest most of the time, we'd all be in trouble. So we strive to be honest. When we are dishonest, we feel off track because we've violated one of those guidelines that most people try to follow. Other commonly held principles include fairness, excellence, humility, courage, trustworthiness, selflessness, respect, patience, responsibility, commitment, and consistency.

These are traits that most people aspire to imprint on their character. Few of us succeed in being all those things all the time. After all, only God is perfect, right? But when you strive each day to be fair, to be your best, to be humble, courageous, trustworthy, selfless, respectful, patient, responsible, committed, and consistent, you build strength of character.

It's important to realize that building a strong character will help you deal not only with the hard times, but also with the good days. There are many people who achieve success, but because they lack strength of character, they don't feel worthy. They may look great on the outside, but they are weak and fearful on the inside. Often, they end up sabotaging themselves because they lack guiding principles.

THE MARK OF A CHAMPION

Having strong character isn't exactly the same as having strong morals. To me, "morals" refers to following certain specific rules of right and wrong—not drinking or doing drugs, for example, or not having sex outside of marriage, or whatever a particular group decides is not acceptable.

Now, there's nothing wrong with being moral. I try my best to live according to my Christian morals. But as I see it, you can follow the rules carefully and still have a flawed character. We've all known people who may not live "moral" lives as some people judge it but are hardworking or honest in their dealings with others. And we've known churchgoing people who would never do anything "immoral," but they still put their own interests above all others. Such a me-first mentality is a strong indicator of poor character. A person of good character puts the needs of others first, even when it's not the easiest thing to do.

Putting the needs of others first becomes especially important if you are on a team. I learned early on in football that my personal goals needed to match up with my team goals. The more yards I gained, the better my team performed. My personal performance had direct correlation to the success of the team. The closer I came to accomplishing or exceeding my rushing goals, the better the Cowboys controlled the clock and the game. And there were certainly occasions when I had to put my own desires on the sidelines to help the team reach its goals. Sometimes when I was injured, I could have easily sat out a game, but I knew my teammates needed me and felt more confident with me out there. So I was there for them whenever it was humanly possible, and sometimes even when it seemed like playing wasn't humanly possible.

Professional athletes are sometimes criticized for having self-centered, me-first attitudes. That may be true of some immature individuals, but I've known many athletes who regularly put the needs of their teammates, their families, and their communities ahead of their own.

And that, I've come to believe, is one of the hallmarks of a champion. I have a few championship rings, and I've known a few champions too. I've never met a real winner in any arena who did not have a strong character built upon well-defined principles that served as guidelines to live by.

Oh, I've known some people who just looked successful on the outside. I've known people who *pretended* to be winners. But the truth will always come out in the long run. The true champions will eventually be known by the content of their character.

Champions don't wear their ideals on their backs like jersey numbers. They live them instead. Because of those core values and principles, the true champions know what they stand for. They know what they stand against. And they choose to stand up for what they believe, putting their principles into action—walking the champion's path.

A CHAMPION TO REMEMBER

I've already mentioned that one of my greatest role models was the legendary Walter Payton. Growing up, I admired Walter Payton's skills as a running back for the Chicago Bears. But as I matured and eventually came to know Walter personally, I saw that the greatest thing about him was the strength of his character. He was a true champion in every aspect of life.

Walter's nickname may have been "Sweetness," but you only have to watch one video of Walter straight-arming defenders twice his size to grasp that he was a warrior on the field. Yet he was always a gentleman and a class act—a humble warrior. Walter had an aura of dignity and grace that inspired me even more than his physical power and agility. To me, he personified the concept of quiet strength. He was a rare man, physically and mentally tough but kind in spirit and warm of heart. He never saw the need to brag or promote himself, because he was so centered, so principled, and of such strong character.

I first met Walter Payton in 1995 in Dallas, during the Doak Walker Award ceremony honoring the year's best college running back. At this point I'd completed my fifth season in the NFL and helped the Cowboys win our third NFL championship together. I'd also just taken home my fourth-straight league rushing title. My football career and my life in general were on track, and I was feeling very blessed.

Meeting Walter that February night took my sense of blessing to another level. His personal warmth and humility inspired me as much as his accomplishments on the field. To my amazement,

Walter approached me, sat down, and made a genuine effort to get to know me as a person. Needless to say, I was beyond thrilled. I'd had dreams of meeting him, but I'd never dared to think we would have an extended conversation, let alone a friendship. I soaked up every word. I wanted to stop the clock and just bask in the moment.

That night my hero told me that he thought Barry Sanders and I were the two players who had a real shot at his NFL record for career rushing yards. You can imagine what his encouragement meant to me. With those words, Walter seemed to be passing the torch. He was honestly rooting for us.

You see, Walter Payton believed in God's abundant blessings. He'd been blessed, and he did not mind at all that someone else might come along and surpass his record. That's another sign of strong character—believing that there are enough rewards on this earth for everyone. Some people don't want to see others succeed. They feel there is only so much pie out there, and they want all the slices for themselves. People like that fear scarcity. Walter embraced abundance.

He wished me luck and told me to keep working hard, and I vowed not to disappoint him. I considered Walter to be a truly great player and a great man, and I felt honored when people compared me to him. There were definitely some similarities. We were about the same size and build, and we both played with all our hearts. But to be the same kind of man he was—that would be a real accomplishment. I respected the man so much I never really thought of surpassing him, only of emulating him and making him proud.

Walter and I stayed in touch after our first meeting, though we didn't see each other for the next year and a half or so. Then, in September of 1996, we played the Chicago Bears, his former team, at Soldier Field. I figured Walter was probably there, but I tried to stay focused on the game at hand. But not enough, apparently. Someone neglected to tell the Bears that we were the defending Super Bowl champions and favored to win this game.

From the opening kickoff, they gave us all we could handle. We were down 10–3 at the half. We couldn't seem to buy a touchdown. We kept fumbling and turning the ball over. Meanwhile, the Bears pulled out every trick in the playbook, including a reverse to a receiver who threw a pass to a running back and a fake punt in which their punter threw a pass.

Injury was then added to insult. With only about four minutes left in the game, I dived over the line on a play fake from Troy Aikman. I jammed my helmet against something, and it felt like a knife jabbing my back. My left side was numb. I couldn't get up on my own at first, so they called out the emergency medical technicians. They were relieved to see that I still could move my hands and feet, but they put an emergency neck collar on me and carried me off the field on a big yellow stretcher.

This was one of the scariest moments in my career. I was lying there wondering whether my football days were over and, even worse, if some permanent damage had been done. *Is this it?* I wondered.

Then I heard someone say, "Emmitt, Walter Payton wants to see you."

Out of nowhere, his face appeared over me. Walter smiled gently, put a hand on my shoulder, and whispered encouragement.

"You'll be fine, Emmitt. You're too tough for this to stop you."

Then he disappeared from my limited range of vision, but I could still hear Walter telling people around me, "Here's my phone number. If he needs anything, whether it's clothes, a place for his family to stay—anything—just call. And please keep me informed too. I want to know how he's doing, but I think he'll be fine."

My injury proved to be minor, and what I most remember about that scary day was the fact that the great Walter Payton came down to check on me, encourage me, and offer his assistance. We'd only met one time, more than a year before. At that point, I was just another young running back chasing his record, yet he went out of his way to show kindness and concern for me. I already had great admiration for Walter as a person and as a player, but after that day, I was in awe of his character.

After that game, Walter and I talked more often. Then, in February of 1999, he called and told me he had a rare liver disease that might require a transplant. He didn't want me to learn of his illness from anyone else. That was just like him. At a time when many people would be consumed by their own fears and concerns, he wanted to reassure me. I don't know how many friends he called to alert that day, but I was honored to be on the list.

Tragically, a transplant was not possible. Cancer had spread from Walter's liver throughout his body, making him ineligible to receive a donated liver. Even though he was sick and fighting for his life, Walter still found the time to do public service announcements to encourage organ donation.

Like most people, I had never imagined Walter being sick, let alone dying. We talked often in the weeks before his death later that year. He was only forty-five years old and facing the end of his life, but he was never bitter. He never felt sorry for himself. His concern was always for those he cared about.

Walter showed me how to be a champion in life. Then he taught me how a great man deals with impending death. One day, near the end, he called and asked me to help keep an eye on his son, Jarrett, a young running back who was about to start his college career at the University of Miami. I was overwhelmed with emotion over that request. I couldn't imagine what Walter was going through. His strength was beyond inspiring.

Walter called me one last time just before his death.

"I'm going to be okay," he told me. "It's in God's hands."

"If you need me, I'm here for you," I replied.

"Just keep praying for me and my family," he said. "Check on my boy every now and then."

Walter Payton died on November 1, 1999. Admirers across the country mourned his passing. I couldn't go to the funeral because we had a Monday night game against the Vikings in Minneapolis. But there was a moment of silence before the game, and I felt like Walter was watching me from above, just as he had been when I was injured at Soldier Field.

That thought left me teary eyed just before the kickoff, but his memory also inspired me. I vowed to honor Walter by playing the best game of my life. I wanted to rush for more yardage than *any* running back had ever gained in a single game. And I nearly did it. I played the greatest *half* game of my career up to that point. I ran for 140 yards and scored two touchdowns just eighteen seconds apart.

Then, only twenty-four minutes into the game, I broke my hand.

Sometimes God has his own game plan. If I hadn't been injured, that single-game rushing record would have been mine to claim that day. I was very disappointed when the injury forced me out, but I still had the bigger record to shoot for, the all-time leading rushing record held by Walter himself.

I've already told the story of when I finally caught up with Walter's record three years later, on October 27, 2002. The preceding July, I'd received the Spirit of Sweetness Award from the Walter Payton Cancer Fund, which is managed by his wife, Connie, and their family. Both were great honors, and though I may have surpassed Walter's rushing record, I will spend the rest of my life trying to live up to that man's character.

Walter stared death in the face the same way he'd stared down so many linebackers on the field. He was fearless. In critical game situations, everyone knew he would get the ball. The defenders all keyed in on him. But Walter ran right at them. He did the same when faced with death. He didn't run from it. He ran toward it with his head held high.

TESTS OF CHARACTER

I have never faced adversity on that level. If I do face it someday, I just hope and pray that God will help me muster at least a small portion of Walter's strength of character. The way he responded to his illness only confirmed what I already knew of him. And even as his life was being taken away, Walter never stopped giving back. This great athlete's death at such a young age and the many tributes paid to him left me pondering my own life and the legacy I want to leave.

How do you want to be remembered when your time comes to depart this earth? Do you want to be remembered like Walter Payton, as a person of strong character who put others first? I do.

I have a few championship rings, and I've known a few champions too. I've never met a real winner in any arena who did not have a strong character built upon well-defined principles that served as guidelines to live by.

We write our own epitaphs every day. They are carved out by the way we go about our daily lives and how we relate and respond to the needs of those around us. I find it helpful, when someone tests my patience or asks something of me that is a burden, to keep that question in mind: *How do I want to be remembered?*

We are all tested from time to time. Each of us must deal with tragedies, failures, setbacks, and hardship. Sometimes it seems like these character tests keep hitting you one after another, day after day, piling on the stress, slamming you to the ground. Just remember that how you respond to the toughest challenges is the true measure of who you are.

Do you cower and claim the victim's cloak, or do you raise yourself and forge ahead, focused not on your circumstances but on your dreams and goals? And how do you act when no one is looking? Do you stick to your principles even when you can't see an immediate benefit? Even more important, how do you treat those who have nothing you want? Can you choose to give even when there's little chance of getting anything in return?

You choose how you respond to those tests, and those choices are sure signs of your character. You also build or tear down your character when you make the choice between telling the truth or a lie, helping those in need or ignoring them, giving credit to others or hogging the spotlight.

CHARACTER LESSONS

I'm not saying it's easy to make the right choices and stay on the right path. It's not. But you don't have to do it on your own. Those who love you will be there for you. God will too. If you stay on the path, you can count on those footprints beside you and under you.

I count myself blessed because God has sent so many people over the years to give me strength and to help me stay on the right path. Any achievements I may claim are thanks to all those who helped build the foundation I stand upon. And the line of people who have served as my guides stretches back to family and friends in Pensacola, the pastors who've counseled me, and the coaches who encouraged me, from Pop Warner football days through high school and college, as well as in the National Football League. It also includes those who've helped me succeed in the business world. All these people were important guides in helping me build my character and find my path.

My first lessons in character building began at home. My mother always held down at least one job, sometimes two, along with taking care of me and my brothers and sister. And my father, always a source of strength, was inducted into ECAT's Million Mile Club—for drivers with that many miles and no accidents. He could have retired earlier, but my father never believed in slacking off.

Pops had his own role model when it came to strong character. His father, my grandfather, worked for more than forty years for a manufacturer that makes flooring, cabinets, and ceiling tiles. To this day, I wonder if my grandfather may have died from asbestos-related cancer.

The adults in my life never sat me down and handed me a list of principles, unless you count the Ten Commandments—and you must. Mostly I learned to value the character attributes that I saw modeled every day in their lives—personal responsibility, hard work, and unselfish love. Still, there were times when they felt it necessary to instill those values in less subtle ways.

I was in the eighth grade when I just had to have some designer jeans. Other guys were wearing them. I wanted those jeans *bad*.

"I can't afford to buy you Jordache jeans," my mother said. "I have to buy school clothes for your sister and brothers, too."

Thankfully, my mom didn't close the door. She wouldn't give me the money, but she did give me the option to self-finance.

"If you want those jeans so badly, you can get a job and buy whatever you want—within reason," she said. "You can come work at the nursing home with me."

My mother was then running Magnolias, a nursing home in Pensacola. Her job title may not have reflected that she was in charge, but believe me, she ran the show. And so I became Magnolias' chief handyman. I mowed the grass, trimmed the hedges, mopped the floors, cleaned the bathrooms, walked with residents, pushed their wheelchairs, and helped them into the vans.

I worked at the nursing home whenever I wasn't practicing or playing football or attending school or studying. The money I earned did pay for my Jordache jeans, but the benefits I reaped from the job went way beyond those fancy pants. I can't say that I always enjoyed the work, but if there was ever a great training program for a future football star, that was it.

I'm referring to *character* training, of course. Putting yourself in service to others builds character. I highly recommend such jobs. Serving as a caretaker to my grandmother and then helping out the older folks at the nursing home really made an impact on me when I was in high school, just as Walter Payton's death did later.

Most teenagers are so busy and wrapped up in their daily dramas that they don't reflect much on the years ahead. I was no different. Yet spending time with people who were nearing the end of life changed me. Some of the residents shared their stories with me, their regrets and failures as well as their proudest moments and successes. Talking with them helped me develop a deeper perspective on my life and a better understanding of my place in the larger world.

I am absolutely convinced that God puts us where we need to be when we need to be there. We don't always understand that in the moment, though. I sure didn't understand it back then. Mowing grass on a steamy Florida day wasn't what I would have chosen to do on my own. Working at the nursing home wasn't as much fun as swimming at the beach with my friends or playing video games. Even so, God must have felt I needed to learn the value of hard work if I was to be successful one day in sports and in business.

I was making a name for myself on the local athletic scene at that point, so God may have put all those elderly people in my life to remind a young guy that the universe did not revolve around high-school football—or around me. Since this was a place where my mother could keep on eye on me, there was no doubt that I would put in a good day's work. At the time, I thought the reward for my labor was the Jordache jeans I bought with my hard-earned wages. The real rewards, as I see them today, were the lessons I learned about serving others and creating my own path in life under God's direction.

I had already begun learning the same kind of lessons while helping to care for my wheelchair-bound grandmother. Did I grumble about having to get up at two in the morning when she'd call me to bring her a glass of water or to help turn her on her side? Sure. I was a kid like any other kid, and sometimes I resented having to do grown-ups' work. But looking back from a more mature perspective, I can see the lessons I learned. And, in truth, I loved my grandmother and knew her needs came first.

The same held true when it came to helping with the elderly folks in the nursing home. I was just part of the team there. They had nurses and aides, but often I was asked to help out, run errands, or see to the needs of patients. I griped about it sometimes, but I learned to be responsible, and I felt a sense of achievement because I was earning money to help pay my own way.

That lesson was brought home one day when my mother needed some cash and asked me to lend her a little money from my savings. I don't think she realized how good it felt for me to be recognized as someone who could make a contribution to our family. I felt I'd taken a step toward manhood and accepted personal responsibility like a mature adult. To this day I don't think the loan was paid back, but let's face it—she has given me a lot more than I could give her!

Years later, when my friend Deion Sanders was named to the Pro Football Hall of Fame, he said that he wasn't playing football at such a high level to win accolades and awards. His driving desire was to provide for his mother so she would never have to work at her hospital cleaning job again. Deion wanted to take care of his loved ones. I felt the same way, and so do most athletes I know. Even as a boy, I wanted to help carry their load. I liked that, and I am grateful for the adults in my life who helped strengthen my character by serving as life guides and teaching me that responsibility is something you run toward, not away from.

MY LAST DANCE . . . FOR A WHILE

Here, too, God was working in ways that would become clear to me much farther down the road. Today's young athletes are increasingly conditioned to look at themselves as commodities and their sports as a business. Some become so focused on developing their earning potential that they lose track of their human potential.

I certainly believe athletes should know their value in the sports marketplace, develop their talents fully, and protect their interests wisely. But I worry that young athletes too often are allowed to think their own needs come first. At some points in life we do have to put ourselves first so we can put ourselves in a position to help others, but there has to be a balance. The me-first mentality will not serve anyone well over the long term.

My parents and grandparents were vigilant about making sure we put God first, everyone else second, and ourselves a distant third. Even in college, the guardians of my character were always in the stands. They were there to cheer me on, for sure, but also to keep my ego in check and my character strong.

My father came down from the stands to remind me of that after a game at Memphis State University in my junior year of college. We had won in our opponent's hostile stadium, and I had a great day, gaining 182 yards. But one thing I'd done that day had not gone unnoticed by my biggest fans in the stands.

It happened after I scored my second touchdown of the day. My teammates surrounded me to celebrate, and I was swept up in the moment. I had never been one to celebrate in the end zone, but my fellow Gators egged me on, so I did a little victory dance. After the game, my father patted me on the back, congratulated me on the victory, and then gave me a little lesson in character.

"Son, I saw your little dance after that touchdown," he said. "You know, you've been in that end zone many times, so you don't need to celebrate and dance like you've never been there before. The great ones don't do that. The great ones act like they've been there before."

Dad didn't make a big deal of it. But once again, in his quiet way, he gave me a gift that I carry to this day. It's funny because my mother was usually the disciplinarian when we were kids. She was more vocal than my father. But when Pops offered advice,

I always listened. I did want to be a great running back, and if the great ones didn't celebrate their touchdowns in the end zone, then neither would I.

That was the last dance of my football career, though I would do some fancy stepping on a different stage down the road. My father didn't object to that dancing at all. In fact, he cheered as loudly as anyone.

OUT OF CHARACTER

Champions have strong character. They may not be perfect all the time or in every way, but they are always intent on being their best. My father and mother taught me that you can't be a champion by simply wanting to be one. You have to have excellence etched into your character. Being your best must be part of who you are.

I'd rather build on success than bask in it anyway. I'm all about moving onward and upward, and that doesn't leave a lot of time for self-congratulations. I prefer to celebrate my victories in small and quiet ways and then look ahead to the next mountain to climb. I've heard that approach called "peak to peak" living.

The truth is that I never felt comfortable dancing in the end zone, anyway, probably because it went against my principles and left me feeling out of character. You generally feel comfortable when you are on the correct path. Even when things are difficult, you still have that sense that you're in the right place. A nagging sense of discomfort may be God's way of telling you that you've gone astray—though it may seem less like God and more like your "gut." You get that uneasy feeling that comes when you find yourself acting in un-*character*-istic ways.

To be comfortable with yourself, you have to remain true to your principles. It's easy to claim them, but how you act upon them is the real measure of your character. No matter what you say, it's what you do that counts. After all, how many boxers say they have the best jab in the business, only to be knocked out by the best hook in the business?

The content of your character affects how you see the world and how you respond to it. Sometimes people bring their own biases and filters to their judgments of you. You can't be responsible for their interpretations, but you are responsible for your actions, especially during those times when your character is measured and tested.

You and I can rise above our circumstances, but we can never rise above our character. We can acquire knowledge and skills, work hard, and live our dreams. But if our character is weak, our accomplishments will not stand for long—especially when we come up against the most powerful character challenges:

- power
- money
- sex

My pastor, Bishop T. D. Jakes, gives a powerful sermon on these three topics. He has moved me with that sermon, in which he says power, money, and sex are not inherently evil. They are simply part of life. Yet they are also extremely powerful, and if we fail to control and manage them, they're almost certain to control and manage us.

These three forces are also interrelated. If you are a powerful person in a corporation or in your community, it is likely that you have money, and it is a fact that power and money have been known to attract sex. It is also true that you can be great at managing one or even two of these three powerful forces, but the third may be your downfall.

This is an ongoing battle, day in and day out. No doubt about it. No one is immune. You or I may be on top of all three one moment and swept under the next. The fact that you and I had a solid upbringing and strong character training doesn't mean we have lifetime protection. (If there is such a lifetime guarantee against human failing, I'd like the full warranty, please.) The only way to stay on God's path is, by God's grace, to know who you are, what you stand for, and where you are in your life journey each step of the way—and to pay attention when you find yourself wandering off course.

GETTING THE MESSAGE

I actually found my way to The Potter's House church and Bishop Jakes at a time when my life was out of sync with my beliefs. I knew better, and I wanted to be better, but in the mid-1990s, I felt I'd wandered off course. I didn't feel lost, exactly, but I definitely didn't have my life together. Part of it was just growing up and reaching a new level of maturity, one that left me yearning for more than the bachelor life was providing.

Don't get me wrong. I was not unhappy with my life. In many ways, I was living my dream. But I was feeling ready for the next stage of life. I wanted to share my days and nights with someone who would love me whether I was playing NFL football in Texas Stadium or in a pickup game back in that old park in Pensacola.

I can see now that God was working on me and within me, sending the message that I had potential to fulfill, but I needed to get back on the right path. I needed a life partner to draw out the best I had to offer. It seemed like the time had come to settle down and start a family, but so far my relationships had not worked out.

But the problem was not with the women or even the relationships.

I was the problem.

This, then, was another test of character. One all-too-common way to fail such a test is to blame everyone around you for your discontent. If your life isn't on the right track, first look within, because happiness can only come from there. If you aren't fulfilled and fully engaged, chances are that the person responsible is the one in the mirror.

I hadn't found the right woman because I wasn't the right man—yet. I needed to get back on the path and do some work on my character.

Some people, especially men, sometimes misunderstand what strength of character means. It doesn't mean that you never acknowledge weakness or that you never let others influence you. In fact, one of the measures of strong character is a willingness to admit when you are wrong. Some people have a powerful need to be right, but that can be a fatal weakness. It takes a true champion, someone of great character, to self-assess, to acknowledge mistakes, to self-correct, and then to move forward.

Believe me, I go through that process often. And I've discovered that there is something liberating in giving up the need to be right. I've taken to living with a learner's permit, being open to what God can teach me through his people here on earth. As I noted earlier, sometimes those lessons are subtle. But sometimes, I've found, God wants to make sure I get the message loud and clear.

A message was delivered to me in just that manner in 1993, when the Cowboys were fighting to make it to their second-straight Super Bowl. One night before a Friday practice, I went to a Las Colinas area restaurant and bar with another Cowboys player, his girlfriend, and her best friend. We'd been there for three hours and it was getting late, so I decided to head home to my nearby apartment.

I'd been drinking vodka and cranberry juice. We'd been talking and enjoying ourselves and not drinking hard at all. I doubt that my blood alcohol level was over the legal limit, but I wasn't paying all that much attention to my drink count. There's no arguing that I'd been more casual than usual about how I rolled that night.

This particular restaurant always had an off-duty police officer or two working security at the front door. As I walked out, I said goodbye to one of them. Then I picked up my Mercedes and headed for my apartment. (How funny is it that I owned a Mercedes but lived in an apartment? What can I say? I was young and foolish!)

I was only about a mile from home when a police squad car came up fast behind me. The emergency lights were not on, but I slowed down.

The officer pulled up beside me and then moved right in front of me. I put on my turn signal to turn right, and so did he. He turned right, and so did I. Then the police officer led me into my own apartment complex. He even opened the gate with his remote control, so I realized he must live there too. But he wasn't going home. He was escorting *me* home.

When I pulled my car into my detached garage, the officer didn't stop to say anything to me. He just kept going and drove out of the apartment complex. He made sure I went home and called it a night, then he went on about his business.

I had dodged a bullet that night. And there were two different ways I could have responded. I could have shrugged it off with an arrogant attitude, saying that the cop was just giving me the special treatment I deserved as a Cowboys star.

Instead, I took the incident as a warning and as a wake-up call.

The police officer had given me a break, I thought. He'd escorted me home, but he'd also seemed to be giving me a warning. If he'd pulled me over and my blood alcohol level had exceeded the legal limit, it would have made headline news and embarrassed my family, the Dallas Cowboys, and my teammates. I would have lost credibility and influence with others. God was telling me that I needed to adjust my lifestyle.

Rather than being cocky and thinking I'd gotten away with something, I respected the moment as an opportunity to learn from a mistake and to make a positive change while I still had that option.

I'd already been through something similar in college. There'd been a big fight on campus involving more than a dozen guys, and

I'd been there. I never threw a punch, but that didn't matter. The headlines read, "Smith and 11 others suspended." My parents were hurt and embarrassed by that incident, and I didn't want it to ever happen again. After the police officer followed me home but did not pull me over, I figured God had done his part.

He'd put me on notice. And notice I did.

BACK ON THE PATH

After that night I gave up the vodka and cranberry for the rest of the season. The only headlines I wanted to make were those announcing that we'd won the next Super Bowl—which, by the way, is *exactly* what happened.

As I continued to take my character lessons seriously, I gradually found myself back on the right path in other ways too. As I mentioned, I began attending The Potter's House and I became more serious about my spiritual growth. Although it took a few more years, I also found exactly the right life partner. On April 22, 2000, the beautiful Patricia Southall became Mrs. Emmitt Smith. She is not only the love of my life and the mother of our children, but she's also a capable partner in business and ministry—and yet another God-given guide for me as I continue my efforts to perfect the content of my character.

I'll never be perfect, of course. Neither will you. But in striving for strong character you will elevate your life and the lives of those around you.

So identify the principles that you value most. Plant them firmly as guideposts along your life's path. Though you may wander off the path from time to time, you can use those principles—and the help of those who love you—to get yourself back on course.

Dedicate yourself to being the best you can be day in and day out. And don't forget those footprints in the sand.

CHAPTER 4

GO ALL IN AND ALL OUT

Commit your actions to the LORD,
and your plans will succeed.

PROVERBS 16:3, NLT

IN 2003, THE DALLAS COWBOYS released me after thirteen seasons. The only professional team I'd ever played for seemed to think I had nothing more to prove.

I disagreed.

So did the Arizona Cardinals, who promptly signed me to a two-year contract.

My competitive spirit was still running high. I did not want to leave football until my tank was empty. Thanks to a workout program that included deep massage and yoga to give my thirty-four-year-old body more flexibility and strength, I was in great shape. I was determined to prove to myself and to everyone else that I could still play the game at a high level.

Arizona coach Dave "Mac" McGinnis saw my commitment,

and he bought into it. The Cardinals had struggled the previous season, finishing 5–11. They needed a running back who could perform at a high level every game. I'd done the job consistently for the Cowboys over the years, and Coach McGinnis saw that. As a Chicago Bears assistant, he had coached Walter Payton near the end of his career, and he knew I shared Walter's dedication to excellence on and off the field.

The Cardinals coach and I had several long talks before I signed with his team. I assured him that I would give it my all in the locker room, the weight room, and the training room, and during team meetings, in practice, and in games. If I signed, I would give it my all. I would be totally committed.

Commitment isn't about sticking with something or someone as long as it is easy or convenient. When you truly commit, you go all in, which means you have to be willing to do whatever it takes, no matter what the challenges might be. You may even hit a wall, but there's no giving up. Instead, you get up and stay with it, doing your absolute best.

Easier said than done? Of course. God loves to challenge those who are committed, but only so we can become even stronger in facing those challenges. That was certainly true for me in this case, because my dedication to playing for the Cardinals was quickly put to the test.

In the fifth week of the season, we traveled to Dallas to play my old team. For the first time in my professional career, I was a visitor at Texas Stadium. If I had any doubts about that, my former teammates made it abundantly clear. They put eight men on the defensive line, and a freight train wearing Roy Williams's uniform hit me so hard I wondered if I owed him money.

Roy's tackle rattled every bone in my body. Lying on the field, I felt like a human wind chime. My ribs seemed to clatter with every painful breath. My shoulder was definitely out of whack, dislocated and maybe broken. But I'd played with worse injuries, so after I hobbled to the sidelines, I told Coach McGinnis to put me back in the game.

Coach wasn't buying what I was selling. Instead, he sent me to the locker room for X-rays. When the doctors confirmed that my shoulder was separated and my scapula cracked, Mac strongly suggested that I sit out the rest of the year on injured reserve.

But instead, I told him I'd rehab the shoulder and be back before he knew it. "Mac," I said, "I came here to help you win, and I can't do that if I'm not playing."

I had missed only four games because of injuries in my thirteen years in Dallas. I didn't believe in coasting, not as long as I could still run. With the help of doctors, physical therapists, and trainers, I did rehab the shoulder. It took me four or five weeks of intense therapy to restore my full range of motion, and then I had to work for a year to build my strength up to what it had been. But I still managed to return and play in four more games that season.

The Cardinals were still struggling. I gained just 256 yards and two touchdowns that entire season—a career low. But I was not done yet.

Coach Mac was fired at the end of that season, but we parted as friends. Years later, he said there would always be "a special place" in his heart for me because I honored my commitment to give the team my best effort. He told a reporter that he'd coached three players who had been elected to the Hall of Fame on the first ballot—Mike Singletary, Walter Payton, and me—and "there's a fiber and a fabric that runs through all of them."

That common thread is commitment, one of the hallmarks of champions in sports and life. Those who are truly dedicated to their goals, to their relationships, and to whatever causes they embrace are most often the people who defy expectations, who make a difference in the lives of others, and who leave a lasting legacy.

My commitment to the Arizona Cardinals did not end when Coach Mac left the team. I returned to the team for one more season, my fifteenth in the NFL. Many sportswriters, fans, and commentators thought I was crazy to still be in the game. They said I risked "tainting" my legacy and that I was "an accident waiting to happen." Most predicted that either I'd be injured again or I'd rarely play.

Their doubts drove me to work even harder. When you are truly dedicated, you find ways to turn criticism and setbacks into motivation. I hadn't signed a two-year deal just to collect a paycheck. I wanted to finish strong. My goal was to work harder than anyone else on the team.

Before the regular season games began, the Cardinals' new coach, Dennis Green, made me a starter. He told the media that I'd earned the job by working so hard in the off-season and in camp. Some people claimed Coach Green was putting way too much pressure on a thirty-five-year-old veteran.

I told the doubters and critics their expectations were so low that all I had to do was go out and have fun. Then I gave them a warning: "Don't be surprised if you see me run for 1,300 yards."

Remember, I was *committed*. Of course, some sportswriters thought I should *be* committed for setting the bar so high, but I came close. In my final season, the Cardinals' "accident waiting to happen" ran for just under 1,000 yards and scored nine touchdowns. I used up all the gas in my tank. I left it all on the field, and I was proud to retire as a player who'd kept his promise. I'd fulfilled my commitment to myself and to the Arizona Cardinals.

GOING AND GROWING

Dreams are built upon your vision for your life, and they provide energy and impetus for what you achieve. You have to see it to want it. What you see in your mind's eye has a way of manifesting itself as a dream. When you write down your goals, then you can act upon them. The principles that determine the content of your character also serve as your guidelines on the path to achieving those goals. The next ingredient, commitment, is important because it keeps you growing and always moving forward. It determines not only where you go, but also who you become along the way.

Proverbs 16:3 says, "Commit your actions to the LORD, and your plans will succeed" (NLT). If you don't commit to consistently working for the life you want to create, guess what happens? You get the life that is handed to you. When you fail to take responsibility for your own life, time does not stop. The world keeps revolving. And very quickly you can find yourself caught up in events and circumstances that are beyond your control.

To commit is to act. Those who aren't committed can only react. If you find it difficult to commit to a particular goal or a job, then go and find another goal or another job—because an uncommitted life is no life at all. It's a life without purpose or passion.

A commitment is essentially a pledge or promise. High-school athletes "commit" to the college of their choice, meaning they promise to play for the school and do their best. But commitment doesn't just mean agreeing to show up. To use a poker term, it's about going "all in." It means going all in and all out, pushing yourself and developing your talents and skills to their highest levels.

A coach once told me that his breakfast plate offered the perfect example of the difference between simply making an effort and making an all-out commitment. "You see my scrambled eggs? Well, the chicken contributed to my meal," he said. "But check out my sausages. The pig totally committed!"

When you commit, there is no turning back. You keep going despite challenges, doubts, and fears. Honoring your commitments often means you give up something, whether it's time, effort, money, or other opportunities. But the rewards of commitment are usually great—not just in financial terms, but in the respect you earn, the character you build, the relationships you establish, and the satisfaction you achieve from keeping your promises.

That's what Coach Mac was talking about when he said that I

would always have a special place in his heart. I did not take the easy way out. I kept my word and delivered on my promise by refusing to sit out the rest of the season and instead working my tail off to rehab my injured shoulder so I could come back and help the team for the rest of my contract.

In my experience, there are at least four major types of commitment you can make:

- To your faith—a love for God and for other people.
- To your goals—what you want to achieve and the work it will take to achieve it.
- To your relationships—the family, friends, coworkers, and community around you.
- To a greater cause—those who are less fortunate and need a hand up, not a handout.

COMMITTED TO YOUR FAITH

I committed to doing my best for every team I played for. However, the most important commitment I've made is to Jesus. I grew up going to church and praying regularly. In college, I belonged to a Christian athletes group. Although I considered myself a person of faith, I was not truly all in at that point. That came later, with maturity and the realization that I couldn't be the man I wanted to be or accomplish all that I dreamed of doing without God's help.

The Cowboys' 1997 season under Coach Barry Switzer was a tough one. We went 6–10 and didn't make the play-offs. There was a lot of drama off the field. We were a proud group of individuals, and it was difficult for us to have a losing season. We loved the Cowboys and Dallas, and we wanted to uphold their winning traditions.

Amid all the difficulty, I turned increasingly to my faith and to my spiritual guide, Bishop T. D. Jakes. I was not alone. (Why do we so often wait for things to get bad before we turn to Jesus?) On October 19, after a tough come-from-behind 26–22 victory over the Jacksonville Jaguars, three of my teammates and I were baptized at The Potter's House church. Deion Sanders, Omar Stoutmire, and George Hegamin joined me in being baptized by immersion. We were making a public profession of our faith in Jesus Christ.

I had originally been baptized around the age of eight or so, but I hadn't understood the full meaning of the experience. As a young man, I'd come to the conclusion that I wanted my faith to be a bigger part of my daily life. Being ministered to by Bishop Jakes had helped me to understand my mission in life and what God had in store for me. My spiritual purpose had joined with my earthly purpose, and that was a powerful experience. My second baptism was an acknowledgment of my spiritual rebirth into a new life. I still had some old bad habits that I needed to root out, but I saw my renewal of faith as a way to make a new start.

It was an exciting day for me—a transformational experience. I felt like I was living the Bible verse from 1 Corinthians 13:11: "When I was a child, I spake as a child, I understood as a child, I thought as a child: but when I became a man, I put away childish things" (KJV). That is how I looked at my life. I was ready to put away childish things and move into mature adulthood.

I'd been doing the same things over and over again and getting the same results, which I'm told is the clinical definition of insanity. By renewing my faith and adjusting my mind-set, I intended to act differently and achieve better results.

Some habits were easier to kick than others. Each one of us is a work in progress, living and learning, taking it one day at a time. Yet after the baptism, I really did feel that I entered a new stage of my life and manhood. I was taking a deeper level of responsibility. I began to see myself more as a leader.

My second baptism was even better because my friends and teammates were there. I felt like we'd been young guys together, playing and having fun, but now we were saying that as men we would be equally yoked, spiritually connected beyond anything we'd experienced on the football field.

Bishop Jakes picked up on that feeling too. After the ceremony he said, "We're excited about what God is doing in the lives of these men. They just won this game, and most of the time after winning a game they'd be out partying. But look what the Lord has done."

Deion and I both talked that day about how the baptism signaled our intention to start new lives. We immersed ourselves in the baptismal water and in our faith. We went all in. We committed to living God's plan, surrendering all to his guidance.

Each of us must find our own way in our walk of faith. For some it takes longer than others. But I am not the first to discover that once you turn your life over to God, nothing is impossible, because whatever you may lack, he will provide.

COMMITTED TO YOUR GOALS

I have sometimes been teased or criticized for being too serious during the football season—in practice, on the field, and even at home. And I admit I can be intense because of my constant striving to improve. When you perform at a high level, people pat you on the back. And that's fine; everyone needs encouragement. But you don't want to get too caught up in patting yourself on the back, which can lead to self-satisfaction and complacency.

I never wanted to be satisfied with just one good game or even one great season. My goals were higher than that, so I had to work at staying focused on performing at a high level throughout my career. As we won Super Bowls and personal awards came my way, I realized that Philippians 4:13 is true: "I can do all things through Christ which strengtheneth me" (KJV). (That's assuming, of course, that I am paying attention to what God wants me to do and following his path.)

I also discovered that the more you achieve, the more you believe that anything is possible. And if you truly believe that anything is possible, then you are driven to push boundaries and break records. But it takes wholehearted commitment.

You have to be all in, totally focused on achieving the goals you have set for yourself and performing consistently, day after day.

A Dallas writer once noted that more than twenty thousand men have played professional football in the United States since the first known player to be paid—William "Pudge" Heffelfinger—received $500 for a single game back on November 12, 1892. I don't have a figure for how many have played since the establishment of the Pro Football Hall of Fame in 1963, but I know it's a lot. But of all those pros, the Hall of Fame has inducted only about 260 people.

Now, I'm sure that everybody who has ever played football professionally is a fine athlete. Players would never make the team if they weren't good at what they do. So what sets the Hall of Famers apart?

The answer is that every person inducted into the Pro Football Hall of Fame committed to always doing his best so that he performed at a *consistently* high level throughout his career in order to reach his football goals.

Consistency is crucial no matter what you do, and no matter what your goals might be. When you dedicate yourself to performing at a consistently high level, you build value into your life. Your consistency works like the compound interest paid to you on your financial accounts. On those accounts, interest is added to principal so that it, too, earns interest. That means that if you can put $1,000 away at 20 percent interest compounded annually, it would grow to $1,200 the first year, $1,440 the second, and on and on—even if you didn't add another dime of your own.

Commitment and consistency can have a similar effect on your investment of time and effort. The longer you keep performing at high levels, the greater and greater the returns. I didn't set the all-time rushing record in any one game or any single season. I became the record holder by fighting for as much yardage as I could gain down after down, game after game, year after year.

Some fans and writers have claimed that I churned out a high percentage of my record-breaking yardage by running the same play over and over again. In the weeks leading up to my Hall of Fame induction, *New York Times* writer Andy Barall wrote that in their glory years, the Cowboys' offensive strategy was very simple: "We're going to give it to the short guy [me] for about three hours . . . and our offensive line and our fullback are going to beat the stuffing out of you until we win."

The Cowboys were known to run the lead draw play about fifteen to twenty times a game. "Watching the Cowboys during those years was a reminder that football isn't necessarily about imagination or creativity," Barall wrote. "It's about doing what you do best, over and over again." I'm all for that kind of consistency.

That's not to say I didn't work on those other aspects of my game that needed work. Certain skills came naturally for me, but believe me, I had to work on being a better blocker, reading defenses well, and understanding the role of every player in our offense, especially my blockers. I learned the responsibilities of my position. Then I committed to knowing what everyone else was doing, including what the quarterback's reads were and when he should call an audible.

All of this was part of advancing my personal goals and those of my team. Throughout my professional career, I was determined to gain four yards every time the quarterback handed me the ball—anything more was a bonus. That's how records are set, how championships are won, and how any life of accomplishment is built—with consistency and commitment.

If you think of a stock to invest in or a brand to buy, you look for those that have been consistently good over the decades, like Coca-Cola, Microsoft, or Apple. Warren Buffett is one of the world's richest men because over the decades he has remained both consistent and committed to a proven investment strategy. He took considerable flack in the 1990s when he shied away from high-flying Internet start-ups. But when that bubble burst, Buffett was again hailed as the "Oracle of Omaha."

WHEN THERE ARE CHALLENGES

Those who are truly locked in to their goals do not waver from one day to the next. You aren't all in if you do your best only when you feel like it, when it's convenient, or when there are no challenges. I never could have set the rushing record by having a big game now and then. The thought of attaining Walter Payton's numbers would have been too daunting. Instead, I dedicated myself to performing at my highest level, moving forward, pushing through obstacles (or finding a way around them), and trying to build up yardage each and every play of every game. You can do the same, whatever your goals might be.

Know that some days you may not do as well as you'd hoped. I had bad games on my way to the Hall of Fame. We all have bad days, disappointments, and slumps. You'll hit a wall every now and then too. The

Throughout my professional career, I was determined to gain four yards every time the quarterback handed me the ball—anything more was a bonus. That's how records are set, how championships are won, and how any life of accomplishment is built— with consistency and commitment.

important thing is to remain committed and to keep striving. If (or when!) you find yourself struggling or backsliding, look for ways to make yourself better, stronger, smarter, more efficient, and more productive. Most important, try to forgive yourself for your shortcomings and learn from your mistakes.

And here's something important I've learned from experience: if focusing on improving yourself doesn't help lift you out of a slump or a downtime in your life, consider focusing on someone else instead. Give it up to God, and reach out to one of his other children—or an entire group of them. I find that when I visit a school, a hospital ward, or a Boys & Girls Club, the rewards are just as great for me as they may be for the people I meet.

One of those rewards is a fresh perspective. I may be thinking that life is unfair, that my challenges are too great, that I'll never reach my goals. But if I look around a little and extend myself to other people, I realize that *everyone* has burdens to bear and that it's *how* we live while carrying our burdens that makes a difference. If I can set my own burdens down for a while and help someone else, I'll come back to my own situation with renewed energy and hope. It's empowering to discover that even when I'm struggling myself, I still can enrich the lives of others.

So don't let yourself be overwhelmed at the thought of what it will take to accomplish your goals or what challenges you'll have to overcome. Instead, take a walk in someone else's shoes. Then commit once more to working as hard as you can, performing at your highest possible level each hour of the day and every day of the week until you reach your goal. Then, once you've achieved a goal, commit to another one that will take you to new levels of accomplishment.

COMMITTED TO RAISING THE BAR

If you are truly intent on leaving a legacy, you'll keep raising the bar on your goals, because if you are not trying to be the best you can be, why make the effort at all? Walter Payton respected Jim Brown as the best, but Walter wanted to be the best too. Twenty-one years after Jim Brown set the NFL rushing record, Walter surpassed it. I respected Walter, but I, too, wanted to be the best. Eighteen years after Walter set the record, I broke it and set the bar higher with the help of many people. But if you think I don't want my own record broken, you are wrong. So, whoever breaks it, good luck and congratulations.

Raising your level of commitment leads to higher levels of accomplishment—as I learned when I first set out to become an accomplished businessman in the real-estate field. As I noted earlier, I chose Roger Staubach as a role model because he was a great football player who had gone on to even greater success with his property-management and commercial real-estate services. Plus, it didn't hurt that Roger lived in Dallas!

Roger welcomed me because he had followed a similar path. In 1971, while he was still the Cowboys' quarterback, he'd started working in the off-season for a Dallas real-estate legend, Henry S. Miller Jr. Six years later, Roger, who had won two Super Bowls for the Cowboys, created his own real-estate brokerage firm, Staubach

Company, which he built into a business with sales of more than $550 million and 1,600 employees.

When I expressed interest in learning the business, Roger graciously opened some doors for me, and I determined to make the most of it. I threw myself into learning this new business.

Were there times when I felt I was in way over my head? Definitely. This was an entirely different world with a whole new vocabulary, and real estate is every bit as competitive as professional football. If I wanted to do well, I had to commit to learning every aspect of the business. I took classes and seminars in real-estate finance, real-estate law, and other related subjects. I put in long hours of study to grasp the minute details of demographics, site selection, and cash flow—all important facets of this complex business. My initial short-term goal was to learn enough to know which questions to ask and when to ask them. Once I knew what I didn't know, I reasoned, I could acquire the knowledge I needed to excel.

I'd had to do that kind of intense learning before, of course. Football at the professional level is more complex than most people understand, and mastering the Cowboys' playbook was not an easy task. But I'd been playing football for most of my life, so at least I'd been on familiar turf when I did that. Real estate was a whole new ball game. Some days I wanted to hardwire a calculator into my brain.

But I kept at it. And by 2005, when I announced my retirement from football, I was ready to launch my first real-estate venture with a company Roger introduced me to: Cypress Equities. Together we formed Smith Cypress Partners. After a couple of years the market turned, and it was time for me to set out on my own. I created ESmith Legacy, a real-estate development and investment company. And I'm just as committed to my real-estate goals as I once was to my football goals. I'm all in—going all out to make my dreams come true. And when that happens, I plan to raise the bar again.

COMMITTED TO RELATIONSHIPS

Most people realize the importance of commitment in reaching their goals. Fewer people give thought to the fact that dedication and dependability are also critical factors in their relationships. To maintain the trust and respect of your coworkers, neighbors, friends, and loved ones, you must show commitment to playing a positive role in their lives. You must also be consistent in how you play that role, how you engage with them, how you treat them, and how you make yourself available to them, as well as how well you keep your promises to them.

One of the things I promised my parents—my mother in particular—when I left the University of Florida after my junior year to sign an NFL contract was that I would return to finish my education and earn a degree. I'd been the first of my family to go to a major university, and my parents did not want me to miss the opportunity to complete my education. They wanted it for me, but they also hoped I would serve as an example and role model for my brothers and sister and for others in our family and in our neighborhood.

It wasn't just my parents, of course. I'd promised myself that I'd get the degree too. I'd always thought of football as a means of obtaining an education and building a foundation for the rest of my life. Still, I might have been tempted to delay my return to the University of Florida campus or not to go back at all if it hadn't been for that promise to my mother.

My financial future was obviously looking strong, thanks to my NFL contract, endorsements, and investments. I probably didn't *need* a degree to meet my long-term goals. But I wasn't about to disappoint my parents. They'd taught me that once you set your sights on something, you go get it done, so I went back and did just that. While most of my Dallas teammates had time for some relaxation in the off-season, I returned to Gainesville so I could complete the college credits I needed to earn my bachelor of science degree.

There were many sunny days when I'd be sitting in class, looking out the window and wishing I was working on a business deal or at least spending time with my friends on the beach somewhere. But I wasn't just playing around. When I was growing up, my parents put schoolwork ahead of everything else. I knew I had to work hard and stay focused like any other student. I participated in many campus activities and even sat in a hallway for three days, selling tickets for a charity event.

I did sign some autographs and pose for some pictures at first, but my fellow Gators quickly grew accustomed to having me around. Then I became just another guy going to class, trying to keep up with the reading and the homework. I guess the one big difference was that I could afford to buy a few extra toppings on my pizza—and my fellow students usually expected me to pick up the tab when we went out to eat.

There was another *big* difference that came up one day in a business-class discussion about legal contracts. The instructor referred to material in our textbook on contract negotiations, and I raised my hand to question it. I'm pretty sure that I was the only person in that entire lecture hall who had actually been involved in negotiating several multimillion-dollar contracts—for himself.

It's one thing to read about contract negotiations in a book, but a whole different deal to sit across a table and negotiate a contract with a shrewd businessman like Cowboys owner Jerry Jones. So I was able to offer my instructor and classmates a fresh perspective, and I sparked an interesting debate on how information in our textbook didn't always match up to the way negotiations went in the real world.

My graduation day finally arrived—about nine years after I'd first enrolled at the University of Florida. I was satisfied to know my college education was now complete, and I felt relieved that I was now free to pursue my dreams without any regrets. The previous season, I'd scored the one hundredth touchdown in my NFL career and I'd topped 10,000 yards rushing. Yet, when I put on that cap and gown and prepared to walk out with my classmates, I was as excited as I had ever been walking through any of the tunnels to start a Super Bowl.

Graduation was a very emotional event, mostly because I was paying back those who had invested so much in me. Sure, I stood to benefit personally from finally having a college degree. At the very least, I'd no longer feel like a hypocrite when I stood in front of school assemblies and urged kids to stay in school and go to college. I was never comfortable making that speech until

I finally had my own diploma hanging on the wall. Still, when I went up to accept my diploma, I felt the day was more about honoring my parents and grandparents than claiming anything for myself.

Three carloads of family and friends drove over from Pensacola for the ceremony. I was especially happy to see my grandfather, Big Smith, in the group. I'd learned many things from him, but the greatest thing he had taught me was the importance of family commitments. For years and years after my grandmother became ill, he would take care of her until he had to report for work. Then the rest of us would step in, taking turns. Her care was a loving family commitment.

My time with my grandmother was often the quietest part of my boyhood. I'd spend a good part of most days hitting and being hit on the football field, playing on the edge of fighting, roughhousing with and manhandling other tough and combative kids. Then I'd come home, walk the few steps across the yard to my grandmother's house, and become an entirely different type of person.

I'd gently feed her a little at a time, putting food on the fork and to her lips, tipping the drinking glass of water carefully so she could drink through a straw. Often we'd talk, and she would share stories from her life. I was a young guy eager to go do my own thing, but it was my responsibility to take care of her. I took seriously what my grandfather often said: "We are family, and we all do things for each other."

This lesson was imparted each and every day in our extended family. My parents and grandparents gave so much to us kids.

They made so many sacrifices, putting aside their own dreams and goals to help us achieve ours. They dedicated themselves to their children and grandchildren, so honoring this commitment to them gave me great joy. On my college graduation day I was excited when I caught sight of my mom holding up a big sign that said, "Congratulations, Emmitt. Proud Mary."

Later, a reporter asked my mother whether she had enjoyed seeing me graduate as much as she'd enjoyed watching me win a Super Bowl with the Cowboys.

"The Super Bowl is a feeling for a little while," Mom said. "But this is something I'll always have."

To me, that underlines the importance of commitment when it comes to relationships. Seeing all my family there, including my brothers Emory and Erik, who were enrolled at Clemson and Florida State, and my youngest brother, Emil, who back then was just graduating from high school, I was struck even more by that power. Sure, there had been times when we fought and competed and frustrated each other, but we'd also inspired each other, driven each other, and cheered each other on.

Jesus provided us with the ultimate example of commitment to relationships when he gave his life for our sins. He gave himself completely for others. This is a concept that often seems lost in modern relationships, especially marriages, which are supposed to be based on total commitment, for better or worse, until death do us part. Many men think what women desire most is material things—a big house, a nice car, diamonds, and jewels. But what most women want is real commitment to the relationship. They want their husbands to give of themselves—their time, their attention, and their support. (After that, most women probably wouldn't mind the house and car and a jewel or two.)

Men and women both need to "go all in and all out" to create a caring and mutually supportive relationship. My grandparents and parents might not have bequeathed to us great wealth or valuable possessions, but they handed down a legacy of loving, trusting, and committed relationships. My wife, Pat, and I hope to pass on a similar gift to our five children and later (much later, I hope) to our grandchildren. We both come from close-knit families, and we work hard at keeping the bonds strong in our own.

I've heard people say, "I never want to be a parent like my own," but that certainly isn't the case with me. The commitment that my parents made in raising us and giving us a strong foundation inspires me. The Bible says, "Start children off on the way they should go, and even when they are old they will not turn from it" (Proverbs 22:6). That's what our folks did for us, and that's what Pat and I want for our five children.

We've worked to make our house a soft place to land, a retreat where our children know they will always find love and support. One of the most important parenting lessons I've learned is to always listen to my children. What they want to talk about may not always seem important. But by listening even then, we keep the lines of communication open—and they'll still be open when important matters do come up.

Of course, we have to be the rule makers and the rule enforcers, too. That's a role we take seriously because we believe all children need to know where the boundaries are, what is right and wrong, and what is expected of them. We are not perfect parents, if such beings exist. Our children are not perfect either. But we are all committed to being the best family members we can be, and we believe that as long as we remain committed to each other and consistent in our approach, we'll be fine.

COMMITTED TO CONNECTING

My most important relationship commitments, of course, are to my family—my wife, my children, my parents, and my extended family. I have relational commitments to my close friends, too, especially my teammates and my brothers and sisters in Christ. But I have also come to believe that a commitment to relationships involves more than just a commitment to specific people. It also means choosing to be *relational* in the way we interact with others. It means choosing to connect instead of disengage, to treat those we meet every day in a personal, caring way.

People remember those who pay attention to them, who make them feel important and significant. Yet this is increasingly rare. We live in a crazy world of electronic distractions that includes cell phones, text messages, and tweets. I can't help but feel, when I'm talking to certain people, that they are far more interested in texting another person miles away than talking with the actual person standing in front of them. That's not a good feeling, because it signals that there is little commitment to the relationship. But we can all work on these things, including me.

Sportswriter Rick Reilly offered an example of this in a column he wrote in 2011 about another NFL player. I found it interesting that one of the anecdotes focused on the hurt that a teammate felt when this other player, then a rookie, kept texting on his smart-phone while the veteran was trying to explain pass coverages to him. According to Reilly, the veteran became so angry at this behavior that he finally slapped the phone out of the rookie's hands.

This reaction is an example of the hurt most people feel when their efforts to communicate with another person are spurned. To fully engage in a conversation or a relationship, you have to commit to interacting with the other person. That means you listen as well as talk, you make eye contact, and you try to understand not only the words but also the emotions behind them.

Why does all that matter? Actions speak louder than words. If you want to be thought of as someone who cares, you must demonstrate that you care. You must make a commitment to pay attention to people and to treat them with care and respect.

One of the most popular athletes of all time, Earvin "Magic" Johnson, was known as a player who gave everything he had on the basketball court. In his playing days and today as a successful businessman, Magic is also known for making the person in his presence feel as though he or she is, in that moment, the most important person in his life. I've experienced this with him, and I've heard others say the same thing. I know that Magic usually has a lot on his mind and many people vying for his attention. Yet he has the ability to commit to one-on-one interactions and con-versations so that the other party feels totally engaged with him.

I may not always succeed in this area of my life, but I try very hard to because I've seen how powerful it can be. I pray that at the end of my life, people will remember me for consistently being "all in" when I meet people, making the effort to connect and making them glad they've met me.

COMMITTED TO A GREATER CAUSE

I stepped way out of my comfort zone and worked my tail off to win the championship on the reality show *Dancing with the Stars*, which I'll write more about in another chapter. After that achievement, I hung up my dancing shoes.

Performing on the show and winning the competition with the talented Cheryl Burke was a lot of fun. Once I'd trained and felt comfortable with each routine, I flat-out enjoyed the performances. Many fans had voted for us because they saw we were having such a good time on the dance floor. But once that party was over, I wanted to return to being a businessman. I wasn't interested in continuing as an entertainer.

As you might imagine, though, after winning the competition, I received many invitations to dance on other television shows, in commercials, and at events. One dance invitation even came during a January 5, 2009, concert in Dallas. I took Pat to see Celine Dion at the packed American Airlines Center, and early in the show, Celine's camera crew showed Pat and me in the crowd on the arena's big screen. The audience kindly applauded us. Celine, being very gracious, responded by congratulating me on winning *Dancing with the Stars*. Then she invited me up onstage to dance with her.

I told Celine that the jeans I was wearing were too tight for dancing. That was true, but it wasn't the real reason I politely declined. This was Celine's night, and I didn't want to interrupt the flow of her performance. And I'd also learned that to look natural as a dancer, I have to put in weeks of practice. Otherwise, well, let's just say I'm no Usher. I had no interest in making a fool of myself in front of that packed crowd.

The truth is, I wasn't looking for a long show-business career, and I wasn't really interested in any kind of dancing except with my wife. But then I received an invitation that was difficult to turn down. Lisa Blue Baron is a prominent Dallas trial lawyer, a political activist, and the widow of Fred Baron, who was also a well-known litigator. Fred had died in 2008, unfortunately, but Lisa vowed to continue one of their favorite holiday events, an annual Christmas party at their Dallas home. This party, which is a big social event each year, also serves as a fundraiser for Lisa's favorite charities.

Lisa and Fred loved to dance together, and they had a tradition of starting each party by doing a big dance number for all their guests. Rather than end the tradition after Fred's death, Lisa began asking one of her male guests each year to dance with her. She requested that I dance with her for the 2010 Christmas party at her home.

That was an offer I didn't want to refuse because helping others and passing on the blessings I've received is a big priority for me. It's something I learned from my parents and something that is built into my faith commitment. Pat and I have even established Pat & Emmitt Smith Charities to support our commitment to a large cause and help others. (I'll talk about that more in chapter 10.)

I wanted to support Lisa and her fundraising efforts, too, so I agreed to dance with her. But I insisted that we needed to practice first.

Lisa, who had been a big fan of my *Dancing with the Stars* appearances, didn't think that was necessary. "I know you can do it," she said. "After all, you won the biggest competition out there."

But as noted earlier, I need to practice and practice some more to nail any dance routine that's going to be seen by anyone other than my wife and a few friends. Lisa's parties are major events covered in the media, so this definitely qualified as a public performance. Lisa was constructing a twelve-thousand-square-foot party tent in her backyard, complete with professional lighting and a stage for live performances.

Did I mention that the acts she'd lined up to perform after our little dance number included Sheryl Crow, Steely Dan founder Donald Fagen, Michael McDonald of the Doobie Brothers, and Boz Scaggs? I sure didn't want any of them or the 1,800 other guests going home that night saying, "That Emmitt Smith really isn't all that good when he's not dancing with Cheryl Burke."

So I agreed to dance with Lisa Blue Baron if she'd agree to dedicate herself to serious practice time. I also suggested that we hire a professional choreographer and dance instructor. "I don't want your guests to be disappointed in me," I told her. "And to be good, I have to work at it. You don't want me stepping on your toes, do you?"

Over three or four months, we developed and refined a routine that began with an elegant fox trot to a recording of Frank Sinatra singing "Come Fly with Me," then progressed after a few minutes into the more upbeat "U Can't Touch This," by M. C. Hammer.

When we hit the part about "Hammer Time," Lisa and I threw off our jackets and moved into a freestyle hustle dance that really gave the performance a fun and dramatic kick. It also required more practice than either one of us had anticipated. As the party date drew closer, we were still perfecting our performance for several hours a couple of times a week.

Lisa and I were game for all the hard work because we were both committed to raising money for her charities and to entertaining the donors. More than $200,000 was donated that night, and Lisa matched that figure. The primary recipient of the donations was her late husband's favorite charity, the Walden Woods Project. Founded by rock singer Don Henley, this nonprofit honors the legacy of writer and philosopher Henry David Thoreau through conservation, education, research, and advocacy.

Dancing for Lisa's big party turned out to be a very big commitment to a cause, to a friendship, and to my own goal of always giving everything my best effort. We had great fun that night because we had our dance number down and could simply enjoy the moment. That meant that the crowd enjoyed it too.

Commitment requires work, but there are always rewards as well. I encourage you to bring all your talents and give all you have to those four areas of commitment—your faith, your goals, your relationships, and your greater causes. When you go all in, you build a life of consistent achievement and, even better, complete fulfillment because you always know that you've done your best.

CHAPTER 5

TAKE FEAR OUT OF THE GAME

The LORD is my light and my salvation;
whom shall I fear?
The LORD is the strength of my life; of
whom shall I be afraid? . . .
Wait on the LORD: be of good courage,
and he shall strengthen thine heart.

PSALM 27:1, 14, KJV

WHEN OUR DALLAS COWBOYS team faced the New York Giants in the last regular game of the 1993 season—actually played on January 2, 1994—there was a lot at stake. The winner would secure home-field advantage for the play-offs, not to mention a first-round bye, which meant a week's rest. The pressure was on.

For me, there was another motivational factor. The season's rushing title was also at stake. I'd won it the two previous seasons, but at that point I was in a tight race with Jerome "The Bus" Bettis of the Los Angeles Rams, and he had just pulled ahead of me. One of my big legacy goals was on the line.

We met in Giants Stadium in the Meadowlands Sports Complex on a frigid day. The field's artificial turf always felt harder than most, but on that day it was like glacial ice, cold and unforgiving. I found out just how unforgiving a couple of minutes before halftime, when Giants safety Greg Jackson tackled me and rode me to the ground after a 46-yard run. With Greg's full weight bearing down on me, my right shoulder slammed into that frozen turf.

Pain shot through my body like I'd never experienced.

The impact had torn the ligaments in the shoulder, separating it. Somehow I also bruised my sternum, which sent spasms up the middle of my back to my trapezius muscles. Worst of all, I could barely raise my right arm. Just taking a breath was difficult.

I went to the sideline to have my injury checked out, but the doctors and trainers said there was nothing they could do for me right away except take me in for X-rays. My upper body was beaten up and bruised, but I could still run. And I knew this was a must-win game. If we lost, we had to play again in a week. If we won, we had two weeks' rest before the play-offs. I needed that rest, and so did my teammates. I was not about to remain on the sidelines.

I did have to make one major adjustment because of my injuries. Upon returning to the huddle, I asked our offensive linemen to make sure someone followed me down the field on every play because I was having a difficult time getting up off the ground and I needed assistance.

Seriously, I was like the old woman in the commercial who says, "I've fallen and I can't get up." Every time I was tackled, I had to wait for one or two teammates to hoist me to my feet. It wasn't hard for them to find me in the pile, though. I could be easily spotted because I was the guy on the bottom. And each time it felt like someone was shoving hot coals up through my shoulder. It hurt so badly I bit through my mouthpiece.

Our quarterback, Troy Aikman, had to make an adjustment for his one-armed running back. My left arm was the arm I carried the football in most of the time, so he had to bend down and tuck the ball into it on handoffs since my right arm couldn't brace it. But I stayed in the game, and I kept running.

My battered chest was so sore that between plays I'd take big, deep breaths to pull air into my lungs. One of the coaches must have noticed, because someone sent in my backup, Lincoln Coleman. But when Lincoln tapped me on the shoulder, I told him to go back to the sideline.

At halftime, our team doctors went to work on me like a pit crew at the Daytona 500. Dr. Robert Vandermeer and our trainer, Kevin O'Neill, did what they could. They gave me two Vicodin to ease the pain, but the damage was too severe to repair then and there.

"Emmitt, it's going to hurt, but you can't damage it any more than has already been done," Kevin told me.

I was hurting so badly at that point that if the custodians and the parking attendants wanted to treat me, I was willing to listen. The Cowboys' equipment manager, Buck Buchanan, and his assistant, Mike McCord, devised a *MacGyver* approach for my aching shoulder. They cut a doughnut hole in the middle of a foam knee pad and taped it to my separated shoulder under my shoulder pads to help disperse the impact of any direct blows to the injured area. Their improvised shield helped some, but every time I went down, there was still a crunching sound in my chest. It sounded like someone was cracking his knuckles in there.

After being tackled on one play, I was in so much pain that I just stayed down. Michael Irvin came over to help me and said, "Hey, man, you have to stay in the game. We need you out here."

Vicodin or no Vicodin, I was in pain, but Michael was right. I had to stay focused on picking up yards and scoring.

This was one of those games where mental toughness was a key factor. The Giants were piling on me and taking shots at my shoulder because they knew I was hurting. My teammates saw that and did what they could to protect me, pulling defenders away from me and off me. They respected me for staying on the field, and they seemed to intensify their efforts too.

In every huddle, Troy would look at me after calling the play and say, "Emmitt, are you all right?"

At one point early in the third quarter, I noticed that they weren't giving me the ball as much. They were using me as a decoy in pass-action plays. I told the coaches that if they were going to put me in the game, they needed to give me the ball and let me run. So they went back to handing me the ball and throwing it to me too. I still don't know how I caught it with one arm, but somehow I did.

The score was tied when the final second ticked off the clock. The game went into overtime, and I did too. Bruised, beaten, and battered, we all just kept rolling. I carried the ball thirty-two times that day even though my teammates all but carried *me* back to each huddle. With a lot of help from my blockers, I managed to run for 168 yards, catch ten passes for another 61 yards, and score our only touchdown.

In what turned out to be my last run of the game, the Giants' linebacker Lawrence Taylor came at me like a runaway truck. Somehow my injured right arm rose up, and I straight-armed him. I don't know who was more shocked, Lawrence or me, but that last run put the Cowboys in position for the field goal that finally won the game.

Then the stuff hit the fan—or at least the pain really hit me. I managed to smile in the locker room when it sank in that we would have two weeks off before the play-offs. Someone helped me pull off my shoulder pads, and I stood up, feeling good about the game. Then I dropped like a sack of potatoes. Spasms ran through the muscles in my chest all the way up to my neck, constricting them so much that I couldn't breathe. I felt as if a giant python had wrapped itself around my upper body and was squeezing me. I was in agony. My teammates carried me into the training room, and the team doctor gave me another shot.

I was lying there on the stretcher when John Madden appeared over me. That was a shocker. The coach-turned-sportscaster patted me on the shoulder and said he'd never come down into a locker room after broadcasting a game, but he wanted to tell me, "That was the gutsiest performance I've ever seen."

Even with all the pain wracking my body, I had to smile at that. I couldn't raise my arm enough to shake John's hand, but I was grateful to him for stopping by and offering that amazing compliment. He said the same thing over and over again in his broadcasts after that game, and I appreciated every word.

Truth be told, if that Giants game had gone another minute, I might just have collapsed on the field and turned to pure dust. Physically and mentally, I was drained dry. I'd given everything I had and then burned up everything in the reserve tank.

The pain meds kicked in, and I was in la-la land when my parents came in to congratulate me. We talked for a while, but the pain was starting to mount. They walked me to the team bus, and my mother said she knew I was in pain.

The pain came with a vengeance as we traveled, and so did the muscle spasms. The team doctors had me lie down on a seat near them so they could keep an eye on me. That was a good thing, because after more meds finally put me to sleep, I woke up in a panic. My arm was on fire. The darn thing hurt so badly that I started banging the arm against the plane window, trying to break it off to stop the pain.

Pile on! My teammates pinned me down so the doctors could hit me with another needle. That knocked me out, but only for a short time. Again the burning sensation shot through my arm, and my own hollering woke me up in a wild frenzy. They offered to land the plane right then and there so I could go to a hospital, but I told them, "If I'm going to die, I want to die in Dallas!"

When we finally landed in Dallas, the doctors took me directly to Baylor University Medical Center and hooked me to an IV bag full of a powerful painkiller. When the meds first hit me, I felt a wave of elation. I was smiling and accepting compliments. The television in my room was turned to ESPN, and when a recap of our game came on, I thought, *Great. I can watch the highlights.*

I didn't see a single one. The mighty meds kicked in fully, and it was nighty-night for this beat-up Cowboy.

THE BIGGEST BATTLE

I remained on that IV through the night. And as exhausted, bruised, and swollen as I was in the days that followed, I felt deep satisfaction, too. With God's help, I had dealt with the pain and helped my teammates win the game they deserved to win. I had also won the rushing title for a third-straight season, too, which was pretty gratifying. (Nice try, Bus!)

I was grateful for those who had made it possible for me to make it through. Norv Turner, the offensive coordinator, let me have the ball, and my teammates blocked for me. They raised me to my feet when I could not pick myself up. On that field they were my brothers in battle for every yard gained.

But try as they might, my teammates could not protect me from the biggest battle I had faced in that game—my battle with fear.

I'd been running scared on that field that day—no doubt about it. I was afraid of losing. I was afraid of being hurt seriously and maybe even having to leave football. I was afraid of letting down my teammates and disappointing my coaches and not reaching my goals.

So my greatest satisfaction after that game was not that I'd played well, not that I'd played with pain, not even that I hadn't let the team down . . . but that I'd been able to manage my fear.

I was surrounded by Giants intent on knocking me out of that big game, but my fears could just as easily have put me on the sidelines. That's a reality we all face. Each of us has challenges that come at us from the outside and from within. You can defeat rivals and overcome challenges at work and in your personal life, but if you can't manage the fears and doubts you harbor inside, you may never be all God intended you to be.

A WARRIOR'S HEART

So far, in our walk together, I've encouraged you to dare to dream, to turn those dreams into goals and to pursue them, to define yourself with strong principles to live by, and to commit to doing your best every day. Each of those elements is essential for you to develop your God-given gifts to their highest levels so that you can fulfill his plan for you. But learning to manage fear and doubt is just as crucial because how we handle our fears will have a lot to do with whether we keep moving toward our goals or get stopped in our tracks.

Fear comes in many forms. There's the natural fear that arises when we face harm or disaster or the unknown. There's the fear of failure and the fear of success, too. How many people do you know who achieve great things and attain success on many levels but then sabotage themselves because they don't feel prepared or worthy of success? Other fears include fear of pain or embarrassment, fear of commitment, and the fear of death.

All these fears have the power to paralyze us and cripple us. But they can also spark the fires that drive us to accomplish great things. The difference lies in how we choose to respond to our fears.

People talk about conquering their fears, but that is not possible because fear is a survival tool hardwired into each of us. We all experience it, so there's no shame in it. In fact, it's there for our benefit. When we are threatened, fear arises to put us on alert so we can make the all-important decision to fight or flee.

Ignoring your fears would be as foolish as tuning out the fire alarm in your home or office. God gave us fear for a reason, but that reason was to protect us, not harm us. Fear is meant to send us into action, not to cripple us. In fact, if we allow the emotion of fear to paralyze us, we put ourselves in even greater jeopardy. We should acknowledge and listen to our fears, but use them as God intended, as a force for positive action.

During that Giants game, there was the war on the field around me and then the war within me. Both were all-consuming, and I was completely caught up in using my fears—my fear of failure, my fear of pain, my fear of further injury—to drive myself toward the goal line. I was so focused on my interior dialogue that I had almost no awareness of the fans or anything beyond what was happening on the field. So I was a little surprised when, after that game, fans and sportswriters and other players talked about my performance that day as something special.

People treated me differently after that game. For the first time, I was being called a warrior. Everywhere I went, they greeted me not so much as a successful athlete, but as someone who had earned their respect.

The fact that so many watching the game picked up on my struggle that day says something about how we honor those who overcome adversity. And I was reminded once again that when we respond appropriately to our fears and overcome challenges, we become stronger.

WORDS THAT OVERCOME FEAR

When I reflect on that game against the Giants and look at the sources I tapped into to keep playing despite my fear, my memory once again takes me back to the park in Pensacola where I played football as a boy. It was there that I first started playing pickup games of tackle football with my bigger, stronger, older cousins who would knock me down and skin me up, then stand over me saying, "You can't play the game if you can't play with pain." They weren't talking so much about physical pain, though that was certainly part of the deal. They were telling me that I'd never be any good if I let my fear of being hurt affect the way I played.

The fear of being injured can cripple you just as much as a real injury if you let that fear control you. But if you find ways to manage your fear, you can actually use the energy they generate to rise above it and become a warrior and a champion.

My memories of my cousins and their efforts to help me manage my fear came back to me a couple of days after the Giants game. For the first time I realized that I'd been repeating those words from my boyhood to myself. Over and over again I'd heard them saying to me, "You can't play the game if you can't play with pain." My unconscious mind had hit the "play" button and made their words a mantra to help me focus and keep pushing through the pain and weariness.

That game was one of the more amazing "out of body" experiences of my life. I say "out of body" because I don't think I ever could have remained on the field if I had dwelled on what I was feeling physically. It was just too painful. Yet when I repeated the

<< Even as a little guy, I knew
how to mug for the camera.

The Early Years

Before I put on a Cowboys >>
uniform, I ran the ball for
Escambia High School in
Pensacola, Florida.

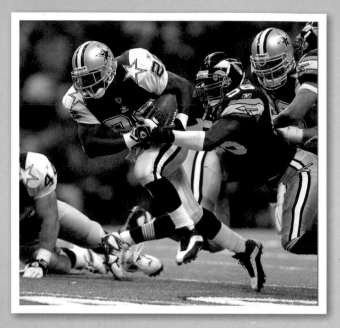

<< Breaking through the
line and away from
Redskins linebacker
LaVar Arrington in 2002

Pro Days

Trying to stay on my feet during Super >>
Bowl XXVII in our 52–17 victory over
the Buffalo Bills in 1993

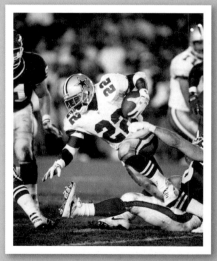

<< Standing with my bust at the
Enshrinement Ceremony for
the Pro Football Hall of Fame
in 2010

I had so much fun dancing and learning Cheryl's routines. It was a hard but incredibly fun and worthwhile experience!

Dancing with the Stars

<< Pat and me on our wedding day, April 22, 2000

Family First

Enjoying a birthday >> dinner for Pat with the kids: (l-r) EJ, Skylar, Rheagen, and Jasmin

<< The newest member of our family, Elijah

words of my cousins, I found the strength to keep running. When I succeeded, my confidence soared. I came through that experience stronger and more certain that, with God's help, I could accomplish nearly anything I set out to do.

That, in turn, reminded me of one of my favorite childhood books, the classic story of *The Little Engine That Could*. This simple tale about a courageous little locomotive that dared to try what bigger engines would not do first appeared as a folk story around 1906. It's often described as a metaphor for the American dream, with all its optimism and can-do spirit. It also reflects my dreams and those of many other people.

In most versions, the Little Engine is described as a small locomotive used in the rail yard to move individual train cars around, but never allowed to pull entire trains. When the bigger locomotives refuse to pull a long trainload of toys and food up the hill to children on the other side, the Little Engine steps up and does the job by repeating over and over, as it goes up the hill, "I think I can. I think I can."

Like many children's stories, *The Little Engine That Could* has a message that is easy to grasp but harder to live. My parents and grandparents read my siblings and me that tale when we were "little engines" ourselves, and I took it to heart.

To me, the message is that emotions like fear and doubt have only as much power as you give them—and it's possible to reduce their power by "talking back" to them. To counter the pain and fear of further injury that dogged me in that big game against the Giants, I kept repeating words that gave me strength and focus. I said them over and over in my mind, and whenever one of my coaches or teammates suggested that I just sit out the rest of the game, I told him, "I can do this. I can do this."

And, as it turns out, I could.

DAVID AND GOLIATH

Since childhood, one of my favorite Bible passages has been 1 Samuel 17. It tells my kind of story, featuring a mere boy pitted against a mighty "champion out of the camp of the Philistines" whose height was "six cubits and a span"—nearly ten feet tall (KJV). The Philistine warrior is described as wearing a helmet of brass and a coat of brass, not to mention brass leggings and a breastplate.

In other words, he looked a lot like an NFL lineman. Ed "Too Tall" Jones comes to mind.

This, of course, is the Bible's description of the mighty Goliath right before his meeting with David the shepherd boy. But little David—an underdog if there ever was one—brought down Goliath with nothing more than a well-aimed stone from his sling and his faith that God would guide and protect him.

I identified with David as a warrior who acknowledged that God guided him in his victory over his fears and his opponents and strengthened him in his weakness—especially in those times when I was being called an underdog because of my size and speed.

To be honest, though, I've never actually thought of myself as an underdog because I actually started out my football career as a big dog. When I began playing as a child, I was one of the biggest guys on the football field. Over the years I became one of the smallest, and I had to learn some lessons about being a David. But I never stopped believing that if Goliath came around, I could take him down.

I was eight years old when I played my first football game for the Salvation Army Mini-Mites team in Pensacola. They assigned me to the six- to eight-year-old division. My coach, Steve Vick, made me the quarterback because kids that age weren't very good at hiking the ball, but because I had big hands, I usually could catch it no matter where it was hiked.

As you might imagine, I was not the classic drop-back passing quarterback. On the first play of that first game, I took my first snap and ran it straight up the middle for a 70-yard touchdown. Coach Vick said that one run became the stuff of legends around the youth league. Soon, everybody was talking about "the kid from the Salvation Army team."

That was probably my first and last easy season as a football player. After that, my size and weight and my age were always a bone of contention. Either I was too big or—later—I was too small. In fact, people who've only known me as a small running back in college or the NFL have difficulty believing that, earlier in my career, opposing coaches and players often complained that I was too big.

Like President Obama, I had a birth-certificate controversy in those early years. No one doubted I was a citizen, but a lot of people doubted I was the age I said I was. I matured earlier than most kids my age, so my mother had to carry my birth certificate to football games. That birth certificate was in and out of my mother's purse more often than her wallet back then because opponents were always challenging me as a "ringer"—an older player brought in to dominate younger opponents.

Looking back, I could hardly blame my opponents for raising the question. I inherited my father's athletic build, with a narrow waist, barrel chest, and thick thighs. It's not that I was just a big kid, but that I was man-big. Even as an eighth grader, I had a full-grown adult athlete's physique. In my freshman year of high school, I reported for football practice weighing 180 pounds and standing five feet nine inches. Little did I know that I was not going to grow much after that, though I did put on another twenty to thirty pounds of muscle at the University of Florida and in the NFL.

Even before my teen years, I was bigger and thicker than most kids my age. You had to be within a certain weight range to play in each division of our Pop Warner league. Other coaches would take one look at me and send me to the scales.

Sometimes our opponents went a little crazy with their suspicions. In our final game of my first year with the Salvation Army team, we played our biggest rival, the Brent Ballpark team. Their coach apparently did not want me in the game against his team. Even after I made weight with my uniform on, he demanded that I be weighed again, only stripped down to my shorts.

That hardly made sense, but he insisted, so I undressed and stepped back on the scale. Once again, I was within the limits for our age group. That really ticked off the Brent Ballpark coach, who said, "It doesn't matter. We're gonna kick your butt."

That was enough motivation for me, but my own coach threw in even more incentive. Coach Vick pulled me aside and promised that if we beat our rivals, he'd take me anywhere I wanted for dinner. We ate the Brent team's lunch, and then I had dinner on them too.

When I was ten years old, the Pop Warner league decided I was too big to play in my own age group. A new coach had me playing linebacker, and in a scrimmage game I broke the finger of one opponent and the tailbone of another. The next day, I was reassigned to play with eleven- to twelve-year-olds in the Midget Division.

I quickly learned that I was no longer the big dog in the new division. One kid hit me so hard that his name is imprinted forever on my brain. Billy Sprague decked me in a tackling drill, giving me an all-day headache and a lingering memory of how much it hurts to be hit hard.

Because I was younger than my new teammates, I didn't receive quite as much playing time on offense, but I went in for trick plays, punts, kickoffs, and defense. I wanted to play as much as possible, so I elevated my game to compete with the older kids. I became more aggressive and tougher so they'd have to worry about me hitting them instead of the other way around.

I relished the challenge of proving myself and learning all the specialty team positions. More important, I also learned to manage my fear and my doubts in order to compete with opponents and teammates who were a year or two older than me. They enjoyed terrorizing the younger kids, but I chose to use their taunts and threats as motivation. They might have scared me sometimes, but there was no way they were going to stop me.

STEPPING UP AND RISING ABOVE

Playing with older kids forced me to work harder. I learned early on that the key to almost every challenge was to put my head down and do everything possible to make myself stronger, smarter, tougher, and quicker. That lesson served me well, because from the time I hit that older group, there was no coasting. I couldn't take anything for granted.

I was often the underdog in the minds of some who thought I was too slow or not big enough. I knew that wasn't true. But since the other kids were just as big or bigger than I was, I couldn't simply overpower my opponents. I had to learn to play smart, to follow my blockers, to cut sharply, and to vary my speed to avoid tacklers. In doing that I became a better football player and discovered talents I didn't know I had. Once again, I had the valuable experience of encountering a challenge, working hard to rise to it, and emerging stronger because I had faced up to it rather than run from it.

That's an important lesson that I've carried from the football field into my business career and my personal life too. Like everyone, I'd just as soon cruise along, accomplishing every goal without any disappointments or challenges. But we all know that isn't possible. You've taken some licks. I've taken them too. And we'll take them again.

No one goes through life without being knocked down now and then. Failures, setbacks, and rocky times are simply part of the package. Sometimes life seems to hit with one thing after another, and it seems the bad days will never end. Frustration and despair can overwhelm us in such dark times. Fears will rise up and para-lyze us if we dwell on them, especially in those times when we are beaten down and just worn out.

That happened to me in 1996. After winning my fourth rush-ing title in five years, and our third Super Bowl in 1995, I just hit a wall. I'd been blessed to avoid serious injuries for most of my career up to that point, but my body suffered greatly in that sixth NFL season. My legs and ankles especially took a beating. It was really, really bad. One night the pain was so great that I kicked off the covers, put my feet on the floor, stood up, and just collapsed like a rag doll. My legs were shot. And that was the night *before* a game.

The physical pain was one thing, but suddenly I was taking criticism from the media, too. There was talk that my career was over. One writer wrote that I had more miles on me than "your grandfather's Rambler." That hurt because I felt I had many more years to contribute and many more yards to gain for the Cowboys. And I was right—but that didn't take away the pain of criticism and the nagging fear that my coaches would agree with the critics and let me go.

I wish there was a magic pill that would ease the discomfort of such times, but there's no such thing. Some drugs may convince you that the pain is gone, but it's still there. I find that reading the Bible provides a far better remedy.

I'll turn to Psalm 23, for example, which reminds me of God's constant presence even in the darkest times: "Though I walk through the valley of the shadow of death, I will fear no evil: for thou art with me; thy rod and thy staff they comfort me" (verse 4, KJV). I find that reminder of God's constant presence even in the darkest times reassuring.

Then in Romans 8:28, we learn that "all things work together for good to them that love God, to them who are the called according to his purpose" (KJV).

I learned all those verses as a boy, and I've learned to live with them in mind as a man. When I hit a rough patch in life, I automatically go to some of those words and tell myself, "Good will come of this. I will benefit from this experience. God will deliver me better than before. All I need to do is concentrate on loving God, obeying his commands, and trusting him with my doubts and fears."

> When dark thoughts dog me, instead of fearing "What next?" I manage my fears by trusting in God's promise of help. I also try to look for the lesson to be learned from the challenge and the good that will surely follow the bad. In doing this, I have learned to welcome challenges rather than fear them.

That is the Lord's gift to us. His words will bring peace of mind to you even in the hardest of times. When dark thoughts dog me, instead of fearing "What next?" I manage my fears by trusting in God's promise of help. I also try to look for the lesson to be learned from the challenge and the good that will surely follow the bad. In doing this, I have learned to welcome challenges rather than fear them.

Challenges force us to grow in ways we might not otherwise do. Without them, we might never test ourselves to learn what we are truly capable of accomplishing. We might never reach our full potential. And we might never understand how much we need God's help—which is an important lesson as well.

Each challenge that you meet prepares you for the next. That's a good thing to remember when you come up against a difficult situation. Calm yourself and manage your fears by recalling how you've dealt with challenges in the past. That's how David summoned the courage to take on Goliath. When King Saul tried to tell David that he was too young to face the giant, David reminded him of his past victories. He told Saul that he'd killed both a lion and a bear while protecting his father's flock. And he confidently said to Saul the king, "The LORD that delivered me out of the paw of the lion, and out of the paw of the bear, he will deliver me out of the hand of this Philistine" (1 Samuel 17:37, KJV).

FACING DOWN FEAR

One thing that has helped me a lot in managing fears over the years is to realize that fears are just emotions. They are feelings. They are "real" in the sense that we do experience them—in fact, we can't help feeling them. But our fears can't actually hurt us or control us unless we let them. They only become a problem when we let our fears run away with us.

Most of us experienced this as children when a tree branch rubbing on the house or a creak on a staircase sent shivers up our spines and kept us awake. The fear then became worse than the reality because it was not the branch or the creaky step that prevented our sleeping, but the images we created in our minds based on the feeling of fear. Too often, as we grow older, we allow our fears to overcome us and even overwhelm us.

I still remember the sensation of giving in to fear just briefly before a high-school football game. We were playing Bartow, a team from central Florida that I hadn't seen before. I was warming up with some teammates before the game when Bartow's varsity squad came in and headed for the opponents' locker room. I was on the weight bench and didn't see them come in, but one of my teammates whispered, "Can you believe the size of those guys? They're huge."

I popped up and peeked out the door. They were the biggest guys I'd ever seen in my life. They had beards and mustaches and looked more like college or professional players than high-school kids. I felt intimidated just at the sight of them. Fear nagged at me as I suited up, and it kept nagging at me as we took the field for warm-ups. Those Bartow jokers looked even bigger on the field.

Then, on my first carry of the game, I took off running. A swarm of their defenders descended on me and . . . I survived!

That didn't hurt much at all, I thought. *They may be big, but they don't hit any harder than any other team.*

I realized that my fears had been worse than the reality. I'd been nervous and intimidated, but not because of anything the Bartow players had done. Instead, I'd done it to myself.

After that, I was like Tom Cruise in *Days of Thunder*. His character, a stock-car driver, wrecks his vehicle. But then he climbs back in it and comes out smoking, determined to win the NASCAR race. That was me after that first Bartow tackle. I went back into the huddle all fired up, and we whipped Bartow's behind. As I recall, we only allowed them to score one touchdown, and we put up 28 points. Best of all, I took fear out of the game by simply choosing to keep going in spite of it.

Some very good players I've known have a slightly different approach. They consciously use their fears as motivation on the field. The great wide receiver Jerry Rice, who was in my 2010 Hall of Fame class, is among those who have acknowledged that they used fear as a force to drive themselves. Some say that they were motivated to work harder and play better by their fears of failing or being defeated or dominated by an opponent. Michael Jordan, one of the most competitive and driven athletes in any sport, has admitted in recent years that he even made up disparaging comments about himself and attributed them to his opponents to motivate himself to play harder against them.

I tend to be more goal oriented than fear driven, so for most of my career my fears were more about not completing my mission or meeting my goals. I didn't have to make up bad comments about myself to be motivated. There was usually a sportswriter somewhere who did that for me, claiming that I wasn't fast enough or tough enough or enough of a team player. I might have considered such critics as nothing more than weeds growing in sidewalk cracks, but they did motivate me to prove them wrong, which I did time after time—with relish.

As a player, my greatest fear was a crippling injury. Like every running back, I had several concussions that were diagnosed and probably some that weren't. The hit I took in the Bears game that brought Walter Payton down from the stands was one that shook me up. The shot that separated my shoulder in the Giants game was another scary injury. Every NFL player is faced with the possibility that one injury or a series of them might end his career. The statistics aren't comforting. The average career for an NFL running back, according to the NFL Players Association, is just 2.57 years.

If I'd chosen to focus on my fears of a career-ending injury, I probably would not have lasted fifteen seasons. Injuries occur in football, and players have little control over that. All we can do is strengthen our bodies and play as smart as we can. I chose to focus on what I could control and developed the warrior mentality of David, the shepherd boy. I managed my fears and doubts by putting my faith and trust in my heavenly Father. Then I fought with all my heart to be the best I could possibly be.

Probably the greatest fears I've experienced were those that would come late at night, later in my football career, when I'd be confronted by my own inner voice asking, *What's next?* Even though I had been preparing for a business career, the prospect of making the transition from football to business was daunting. Would I be able to perform in this new field at the same level that I'd achieved in my athletic career?

I was intimidated over starting an entirely new career, but I was excited, too. My challenge was to manage my fears by using skills I had learned as an athlete—doing what I could to prepare, focusing on my goals instead of my fears, using the fear-generated energy to drive me toward success, and—always—trusting in God to strengthen me and calm my fears as I moved forward into something new.

WITH NO FEAR OF FAILURE

Many people never become successful because they fear failure. They don't chase their dreams because they are afraid they won't achieve them. But how can you ever create the life you want if you don't try? The fear of failure doesn't make sense to me because every successful person I know has failed a time or two. Donald Trump has bankrupted at least one company, but he's still in the game. Successful people understand that failing is part of the learning and growing process.

Football is a great metaphor for life. It teaches you about perseverance, hard work, teamwork, commitment, sacrifices, self-esteem, overcoming fears, getting back up after getting knocked down, winning and losing, and playing for something bigger than yourself. It also teaches you a lot about failure.

As an athlete, you have to deal with failure as part of the game. A baseball player who is afraid of striking out won't go very far in a game where .400 is considered a great batting average. I spent more than twenty-five years playing a game in which getting knocked down was just part of the deal. Sure, I broke the NFL rushing record, but in all those years of running, I probably pulled a ton of turf out of my face mask from falling short of the goal line.

Did being tackled make me a failure? You could say that, or you could frame it another way—that every yard I gained was a step toward success. And I got 18,355 of them, one at a time.

Even lost games and losing seasons are not deal-breaking failures as far as I'm concerned. Don't get me wrong—I hate losing. But I can honestly say I've never lost a game that I didn't learn something from. I certainly don't consider myself a failure because I didn't win every game, and I don't start a new venture worried that I might not succeed. Instead, I try to concentrate on the steps I can take to do well.

Taking things one step at a time is something I first learned as a football player. Football has become an increasingly complex sport, especially at the professional level. Coaches teach their complicated offensive and defensive strategies and plays by breaking them down for each player and then running the team through the plays over and over again in game films, diagrams, and on the field. I've found that the best way for me to master any daunting task is to break it down step-by-step.

As I noted earlier, I was initially intimidated at the thought of breaking Walter Payton's rushing record, but I overcame that intimidation by focusing on doing the best I could on every play in every game for every season. That's one of the best ways I found to handle the fear of failure—to concentrate on the task at hand and break my big goals down into smaller, more manageable steps. It also helps to find someone who has walked the path you want to follow.

FOLLOW A PATH TAKEN

I was still with the Cowboys when Pat and I became friends with former NFL player Steve Johnson and his wife. Steve was a standout at tight end for Virginia Tech and played two years with the New England Patriots before coming to Dallas. A knee injury ended his football career prematurely, but his competitive fire helped make him a success in real-estate development in Virginia.

My wife is from Virginia, and her friendship with Steve's wife brought us together. I'll always be grateful to Steve for the hours he spent explaining the development business to me and helping me understand the basics of net operating income, operating expenses, and cash flow.

More than anything, Steve showed me that it is possible for a former football player to be successful in real-estate development if he is willing to put as much work into the new field as he did in his athletic career. What I learned from him really helped me know what I didn't know, which then gave me the confidence to ask Roger Staubach to introduce me to the Dallas real-estate-development market. Steve and Roger were guides who generously gave of their time and knowledge, and I will always be grateful for them. They encouraged me and helped me manage my fears by telling me how they had succeeded in doing what I hoped to do.

THE ULTIMATE PARTNER

My fears of beginning a new career were eased by Roger and other athletes who had traveled the same path and succeeded in making the transition into the business world. They guided and encouraged me. But of course my ultimate guide and encourager has been my God, who reminds me again and again in his Word that I have nothing to be afraid of if I put my trust in him.

Have faith that whatever you lack, God will provide. Hold on to his hand and reach out to mentors, role models, and guides. Focus on your goals rather than your worries. Break down into manageable steps those big goals that intimidate you.

Know that fear is a natural emotion and a survival tool that should send you into action rather than stifle you. Remember that the fear is often far worse than the reality. And when you find yourself in a challenging situation, go back to those times when you persevered and succeeded.

Call upon memories of achieving victory over your fear, and use those memories to develop the heart of a warrior who always acknowledges God's role in victory.

CHAPTER 6
WIDEN YOUR HORIZONS

Oh, that you would bless me and enlarge my territory!

I CHRONICLES 4:10

AFTER FIGHTING OFF defenders twice my size and grinding out the most yardage in NFL history, I stepped onto a new stage—only to be tripped up by the tango. This stumble occurred after I put my reputation as an athlete and a winner on the line in the fall of 2006 by signing up to compete in the third season of the reality show *Dancing with the Stars*.

My football career had ended with my retirement just a year and a half earlier, so this was quite a leap. And of course the announcement that I was entering a dance competition set me up for all sorts of ribbing from teammates, opponents, and friends. One of my closest friends said he could not bear to watch me trade my football uniform for dance wear.

"Emmitt, I love you, man, " said Tim Brown, the former Oakland Raider, "but I don't ever want to see you in tights."

Others feared that I might make a fool of myself. Even my wife, who loves to dance with me, expressed her doubts. "Why would you want to go on that show? You've never done ballroom dancing. Are you missing football and the limelight?"

A man can always count on his woman to ask the tough questions!

No, I didn't miss the limelight. I am not an attention junkie, nor am I a slave to celebrity. I had no inner need to be on television. And my business interests were keeping me plenty busy. In fact, I'd turned down the *Dancing with the Stars* producers when they asked me to compete during the show's first two seasons.

My pastor often reminds us that God may not show up when you want him to, but he is always right on time. So I've come to believe we should welcome opportunities when he presents them. Don't say, "It's not a good time" or "I'm too busy." Instead, thank God for opening a new door. Sometimes you may decide to walk through it even though you don't know where the path will lead you—because God knows. He opens and closes doors for his divine reasons. If an opportunity seems to match up to your talents and your purpose, why not put your trust in him and take a risk?

After watching my friends Evander Holyfield, Master P, and Jerry Rice compete on *Dancing with the Stars* in the first two seasons, I thought, *I couldn't do any worse than they did!* By its third season the show had become very popular, and other athletes had competed without destroying their reputations, even when they wore tights and high-heeled shoes.

So when the producers called me again, I decided to strap on the dancing shoes and give it a shot. I thought being a contestant would provide me with a great opportunity to introduce myself to a larger audience and maybe to expand my business and media opportunities beyond sports.

In 1 Chronicles 4:10, the Bible says God granted the request of Jabez when he prayed, "Oh, that you would bless me and enlarge my territory!" There are many opinions on that particular passage and how to interpret it, but my take is that Jabez was asking his heavenly Father to help him widen his horizons by granting him opportunities to develop his God-given gifts so that he might better serve the Lord's purpose and be a blessing to others.

You and I are only on this planet for a brief visit. God has a purpose for our lives and has given us the gifts we need, including our time and our talents, to pursue and fulfill that purpose.

Your vision fuels your dreams. Your goals define your purpose and send you into action. Strength of character, unrelenting commitment, and the courage to manage your fears carry you through the challenges. To fulfill your highest purpose, though, you must ready yourself, then recognize and act upon the opportunities God presents you.

Some opportunities may be related to your career or your finances. Others may involve your relationships, your ability to serve others, or the power of your faith. As a person of many facets, you are capable of extending your reach in many directions. And I believe God wants you to do that. He wants you to stretch and to grow, to welcome big breaks and tipping-point moments that set you free to flourish in new fields and in new ways. It is our responsibility to make every minute count and to multiply our gifts not just for our own benefit, but also for the greater good and to glorify his name.

But if we're going to do that, we have to pay attention—so we'll notice the opportunity when it arrives.

DON'T GET DISTRACTED

Ephesians 5:15-16 cautions us to put our time on earth to good purpose, being careful to live "not as unwise but as wise, making the most of every opportunity, because the days are evil." Bible scholars say that, in this case, "evil" refers to distractions that can keep us from developing our gifts, honoring God, and serving others.

As I mentioned in chapter 4, the distractions that bombard us today are beyond anything the authors of the Bible might have imagined, thanks in no small part to television, personal computers, video games, smartphones, iPads, and the Internet. If we aren't talking on our cell phones or checking our text messages and our e-mail, we are texting or tweeting, updating our Facebook statuses, browsing YouTube, or googling this and that. Several studies have shown that young people who spend hours jumping from one of these distractions to the next have increased difficulty studying, processing, and retaining information. Adults can also become addicted to texting, checking e-mails, and jumping on the Internet to the point where they become less productive at work and at home.

Technology can be a blessing when it informs and educates us, but it can also cause us problems when it lures us away from other more productive activities. I worry about the obesity rates among young people who don't run around and play outside like we used to because they are playing video games instead. We have so many distractions that we sometimes forget to take care of ourselves and our responsibilities. Even worse, we could easily fail to recognize and take advantage of opportunities that come our way.

To be all that God wants us to be, we have to stay focused and alert, ready to take advantage of new opportunities and multiply our blessings when given the chance.

SELF-SABOTAGE

Smartphones, laptops, iPads, and PlayStation PS3s aren't the only hindrances that can keep us from recognizing and taking full advantage of opportunities that come our way. Often we sabotage ourselves when we become focused on short-term and selfish goals that blind us to much greater possibilities ahead. The Bible offers many examples of people who missed out because they were short-sighted and self-involved. One of the most well known of these is the parable of the talents in Matthew 25:14-30 (KJV).

In ancient times, a "talent" was a unit of weight used to measure gold or silver. This parable tells of a wealthy man who was going on a journey and called his servants together beforehand. He gave his most valued servant five talents. A second servant received two talents, and a third, just one. The most valued servant invested his five talents and earned five more. The second servant also doubled his talents. But the third servant buried his one talent because he feared being punished if he did not still have it when the wealthy man returned.

When the man came back, all three servants told him what they had done with the money, and they returned to him all that he had given them, plus what they'd earned with it. The master praised the two servants who had doubled their share of the money, and he promised them better and more important jobs. But the servant who had wasted the chance to invest the money was condemned as lazy by the wealthy man, who kicked the "unprofitable servant into outer darkness [where] there shall be weeping and gnashing of teeth" (verse 30, KJV).

The talents in this story were a form of material wealth—and it definitely says something about how we use our money. But the point about investing what we've been given applies to our skills and abilities, too—what we commonly think of as talents. How we use our gifts determines which doors God opens or closes for us.

My football talent carried me from Pensacola to Gainesville to the Dallas Cowboys and the Hall of Fame. It has put me in front of kings, presidents, CEOs, and owners of great companies, and I've had an opportunity to learn from them. I've also been able to take that first talent (and others) and multiply it in other areas, including commercial endorsements, the *Dancing with the Stars* championship, my own real-estate-development and construction firm, and our charitable foundation.

I didn't bury my talent in the ground, thinking that football would carry me through life. As an athlete from humble beginnings, I was blessed with opportunities to be a change agent for myself, my loved ones, and those who benefit from my business ventures and my charities. I encourage other athletes and all people to multiply and maximize their gifts.

I don't know about you, but I wouldn't enjoy being cast out into the darkness where there is weeping and gnashing going on. So I take this parable as a warning never to hoard my gifts or take them for granted. Instead, I must always be on the lookout to multiply them and use them to benefit others.

THE CHANCE TO BE BLESSED

The story of the servant who buried his talent reveals what can happen to those who are too shortsighted or too afraid to see the possibilities beyond the present moment. Another familiar Bible story describes in even starker terms what can be missed when this happens. A passage in the Gospel of Luke offers an example of what may be the ultimate missed opportunity—the chance to ask for God's blessing.

We've all seen the unforgettable image of Jesus Christ in the final moments of his earthly life, nailed to a cross with the two thieves crucified to the right and left of him. One of the thieves, we're told, "railed on him, saying, 'If thou be Christ, save thyself and us.'"

The other thief, however, showed sympathy for Jesus, as a man who had "done nothing amiss." He then took the opportunity to ask Jesus to "remember me when thou comest into thy kingdom."

And Jesus answered, "Today shalt thou be with me in paradise" (Luke 23:39-43, KJV). The two thieves were in the exact same situation in the exact same place at the exact same time. One could not see beyond the moment. He wanted only to be set free from his pain. The other thief saw the opportunity to spend eternity in heaven.

What a powerful lesson that is, and it applies not just to matters of faith and salvation, but also to everyday life. All too often, we miss out on God's blessings because we fail to look beyond the here and now.

STEPPING UP

I saw my invitation to appear on the third season of *Dancing with the Stars* as an opportunity with many potential benefits. I'd just left football, where I was "onstage" twenty-one weeks of each year, performing for millions of people and, I hoped, building a name or "brand" that had value not just in the marketplace but also in the hearts and minds of those who watched our games. That value is important to me because it generates opportunities—not just in financial terms, but also in business and personal relationships, as well as in philanthropic matters and those related to spiritual growth.

When I left football, however, I no longer had that seasonal platform for building my name and reputation. *Dancing with the Stars* offered the potential for a fifteen-week return to the public stage before a much more diverse audience. Tens of millions of people watched the show, and many of them might never have known me as a football player or businessman. Reaching a wider audience appealed to me because I want to make an impact on this world in as many ways as I can, across as many platforms as I can master.

I really thought my involvement in *DWTS* would be fun for my friends and my family, too.

Or not.

"Emmitt, are you *really* sure you want to be on television, dancing in front of millions of people?" Pat asked.

"Are you worried I'll embarrass myself?" I asked.

"No, honey, I'm worried you will embarrass me."

Pat was teasing. I think. She'd always said I was a good dancer, but then wives have been known to fib just to keep their husbands on the dance floor.

Agreeing to appear on this network show would certainly take me a couple thousand miles out of my comfort zone. There was something scary about stepping in front of millions of viewers without a helmet to hide my face. (I asked. They said no headgear and no pads. There would be times when I would sincerely regret that policy.) But I'm a competitor. I enjoy challenging myself. And when I watched other athletes on *Dancing with the Stars*, they looked like they were having fun.

Then someone reminded me that a judge on the show had slammed one of Jerry Rice's performances as "geriatric" and that Master P and his partner once received only an 8 out of a possible 30 points for a performance.

Ouch!

Did I really want to do this after all?

MAKING A LEAP

Every opportunity has its upsides and downsides. I didn't step onto this new and unfamiliar stage without careful consideration of both. I talked it over with my business advisers, my agent, my friends, and my family.

Some thought I was making too big a leap. But in my experience, the best opportunities are often the scariest ones. After all, making a leap requires you to leave solid ground for the open air. Still, you always want to make sure you have a safe place to land.

I dove through most openings that appeared on the football field, but there wasn't a whole lot of time for thoughtful contemplation out there. And sometimes what looked like an opening turned into a three-hundred-pound defensive tackle. The game of life can be like that too. Opportunities can open up in a hurry. You have to decide whether they are right for you by looking at how they match up to your goals, your purpose, and your principles.

So I always try to look before I leap. I encourage you to do that too. Be open to every chance to extend your reach, but know that not every job offer, investment plan, business deal, or social invitation will match up with what you want for your life based on your dreams and your principles and values.

I dove through most openings that appeared on the football field, but there wasn't a whole lot of time for thoughtful contemplation out there. And sometimes what looked like an opening turned into a three-hundred-pound defensive tackle. The game of life can be like that too. Opportunities can open up in a hurry. You have to decide whether they are right for you by looking at how they match up to your goals, your purpose, and your principles.

You may not have much time to decide whether to accept a promotion or transfer at work. A "limited time" offer to invest in a stock or buy a car might tempt you to act on impulse. A last-minute invitation can also be enticing.

How can you be sure you don't make a mistake in such a time-sensitive context?

Well, you can't be sure. Everybody makes mistakes from time to time. But it helps to remember two things.

First, most mistakes are not fatal. Often you can change your mind and retrace your steps. If not, there's always something to learn from the mistake.

Second, you'll reduce your chances of making a mistake if you expect opportunities to arrive and prepare for them.

ALWAYS PREPARED

One newspaper reporter wrote that my *Dancing with the Stars* success proved that "Smith still has the work ethic and determination to ballroom blitz his way to victory after retiring from a fifteen-season NFL career." I would humbly add one more attribute to that writer's assessment. I do have a strong work ethic and a fierce determination. But even more important is the fact that I am always hungry—hungry for new opportunities to grow my gifts so that I can better follow the path God has laid out for me.

I grew up in a low-income situation, but I grew out of it by preparing myself for opportunities and making the most of each that came my way, whether on the football field, on my college campus, in business, in my community, or in the larger world around me. That can be true for you, too. Where you begin your life, even where you are right at this moment, does not determine where you can go. The life you lead is, to a large degree, determined by how well you prepare yourself for—and handle—the opportunities that come your way.

When I first reported for practice in my rookie season with the Dallas Cowboys, I was initially shocked at how much faster everyone is in the NFL. Every NFL rookie has a similar experience. I stood on the practice field the first time, and my jaw dropped at the speed of the action during a scrimmage. It was then that I realized I would have to completely master the Cowboys' sophisticated playbook because the pro game moves so fast that there is no time for thinking, only playing.

I had to be prepared for the opportunity to play because if I made a mistake on the field, both my teammates and I would pay a price. It happens. In 2010, for instance, Cowboys quarterback Tony Romo was knocked out for the season with a broken collarbone when a rookie fullback missed a blitz pickup and gave a Giants linebacker a clear shot at the team's number one guy.

I never wanted to be responsible for a botched play, let alone a teammate being hurt, so I did my best to know my assignments well enough that I was always in position. A defender might beat me physically, but making mental mistakes was a real no-no. It's the same with any profession and with life itself. You have to prepare yourself to do your job properly, to bring integrity to your work or craft, and to respond quickly to what comes up in the spur of the moment.

Part of the challenge facing young athletes is to accept that when you reach the highest level you must become a professional, not just in name but also in your attitude. The same holds true with any young person stepping out of college or high school into the real world of work and responsibility. A professional takes the job seriously. A professional comes to work on time. A professional understands roles and responsibilities and prepares mentally, physically, and emotionally for both.

As a rookie I decided that I had to live up to the professional image by always preparing myself for what might happen on the field. Believe me, there was nothing easy about it, and the grind was even harder late in my career. I'd finish the football season in January, take maybe four weeks off, and then begin preparation for the next season. I pushed myself even in my last two years by getting up at five in the morning for my five-thirty workouts. My regimen was all about gaining a mental edge so that when the other guys showed up at the gym at eight thirty or even seven thirty, they'd see I'd already been there working hard for an hour or two. Word always spread. My teammates and my competitors across the league knew I was committed, determined, focused, and prepared.

It was always important for me to be able to look my teammates in the eye and say, "I would never cheat you." I worked my behind off so they would never have to worry about me getting tired during a game. I studied the playbook. I knew my assignments. Sure, I got beat from time to time. I'd get confused on the field every now and then. But I made sure I knew my responsibilities so that, season after season, I was prepared to play at a consistently high level.

Preparation is the key to taking advantage of opportunity when it arrives. But not every opportunity is as predictable as my participation in a game. How could I ever have guessed that my next major opportunity after football and real estate would be ballroom dancing?

How do you prepare for opportunities you can't see coming?

The best way I know is to keep working on your dreams, your goals, and your purposes. Know what you want, what you value, and where you plan to go in the long haul. It's never a bad idea to get in shape and save a little money. But after you've done those basics, you can relax. Keep doing what you do, and keep your eyes open for opportunities that might arise.

If you've done your homework, you'll be ready to make the leap.

INSPIRED BY FAITH AND FAMILY

Sometimes it's scary to make a move, but you can't be afraid to leave what is comfortable but unsatisfying for what may be challenging but ultimately more fulfilling. I encourage you to carefully assess each potential blessing that comes to you. Then, once you choose to act, commit to your new venture and anticipate greatness.

I embrace opportunities from two perspectives. The first is from the vantage point of my Christian faith and my belief that opportunities are God's gateways to the life he has planned for each of us. The second is from a family perspective.

As I explained in an earlier chapter, historical records found during research for my segment of the *Who Do You Think You Are?* television series proved without a doubt that I am the descendant of slaves. My ancestors were kidnapped from their families and homes, dragged in chains to a ship, and transported to a foreign place where they were traded like livestock and treated as less than human. As a result, they were robbed of nearly all the opportunities normally enjoyed by free men and women.

Slave labor built much of the United States and its early infrastructure. The blood, sweat, and tears of enslaved men and women generated great wealth, yet the slaves were rarely compensated or rewarded. Even after they were freed from slavery, they were denied access to education and the right to vote, generate income, or own property.

My slave ancestors and the African Americans of the generations that followed thirsted for opportunity. They had to fight for their lives and their livelihoods, and eventually they became united in their struggles. Despite kidnappings, beatings, and lynchings, they formed organizations like the Southern Christian Leadership Conference, the National Urban League, and the NAACP. From those groups and from the churches and segregated buses, great leaders emerged. Among those heroes were Rosa Parks, Malcolm X, and the Reverend Martin Luther King Jr., who was assassinated after proclaiming his dreams for his people.

One of those dreams was equality of opportunity.

Those who fought for civil rights often said that they were really fighting for the right to compete on a level playing field. After centuries of being denied that right, they were hungry for real opportunity. Many operated on a principle voiced by another civil rights champion, Whitney Young, who said, "It is better to be prepared for an opportunity and not have one than to have an opportunity and not be prepared."

Because so many before me were prepared but never had the opportunities that have come my way, I am dedicated to being the most productive citizen, father, and leader I can be. I believe we have a responsibility to honor all those who came before us by never taking our opportunities—whether financial, educational, career, character building, or philanthropic—for granted.

Whenever I'm given a shot at something promising, I try to consider the impact on my children and future grandchildren before I make the decision to take that shot or turn back. That's because I am so grateful to my grandparents and parents who worked not only to better their own lives, but to prepare us for opportunities that they never had. My father and mother were not able to attend college, for example, yet throughout my childhood they stressed the importance of higher education. Through their examples and their words, they passed on to me values and principles that prepared me not only to achieve success, but to handle it well and enjoy it.

One of the most important values my parents passed down to me was to never waste time or talents by being idle when I could be bettering myself in some way. As older people used to say, idle time is the devil's workshop. It's a little known fact, for example, that I didn't just *play* football as a boy. I coached it too. When I was thirteen years old, I was enrolled at Brownsville Middle School, which didn't have a school football team. And I couldn't participate in Pop Warner football anymore because the weight limit for my age group was 160 pounds and I tipped the scales at a solid 180 pounds. (No, I didn't consider Weight Watchers for kids because there was no fat on my body.)

I wasn't about to spend that football season sitting around eating candy bars. My parents believed that no good could come of "idle hands and idle minds." Besides, I missed competing with my teammates. So I was very glad to accept an opportunity to be the running back coach for Coach Edgar's team. That way I could work out and stay fit while also learning the game from a completely different perspective. That experience taught me to be open to new, even unexpected, opportunities as long as they are in line with my ongoing purpose.

In that sense, coaching Pop Warner football as a thirteen-year-old was great preparation for dancing on national TV as a thirty-seven-year-old.

Who could have predicted that?

A NEW STAGE

I finally accepted the invitation to appear on *Dancing with the Stars* after carefully watching the two previous seasons. The judges could definitely be tough, but there seemed little chance they could hit any harder than the Pittsburgh Steelers or the Minnesota Vikings. And there was a chance that I could fall on my face, but at least I didn't have to worry about being tackled by fellow competitors like Jerry Springer and Mario Lopez. (Although I'm sure they both thought about it.)

I felt even better about my chances on the show when the director paired me with Cheryl Burke, who had won the *Dancing with the Stars* championship the previous year with former 98 Degrees singer Drew Lachey. Cheryl had been a ballroom dancer since she was a little girl, so I was confident she could hold up her end. I just wasn't so certain she could hold up *me*.

My transition from the football field to the ballroom floor actually started out well. Mastering the routines was a challenge at first, but Cheryl and others patiently eased me into them in our first series of practices before we stepped in front of the cameras.

Even Pat was impressed with my initial progress. "Honey," she said after our final rehearsal, "you are going to surprise a lot of people."

She was right. I even surprised myself in the first two shows. Cheryl and I pulled off the cha-cha and quickstep routines with hardly a hitch, scoring a solid 24 for each of them, which put us in the top three going into the third week of the ten-week competition.

Then, as we prepared for the third week's performance, I discovered a cruel reality of the dance world: it takes two to tango. And one of us was not ready for prime time.

There did not seem to be a tango in my tank. It's a slower dance, and I'm more of an up-tempo guy. I wasn't feeling the tango. I couldn't get into the rhythm of it.

It didn't help that our practice schedule for that week was messed up. I had other commitments that sent me flying all over the country, so Cheryl and I couldn't put in as much preparation as we needed to nail this number.

When the time came to take the stage, Cheryl was ready because she's a pro. I had every confidence in her. But I wasn't all that confident in her partner. If it had been a football game, I would have called a time-out. Unfortunately, there are no time-outs in a dance competition. Whether I was ready or not, it was curtain time.

We danced to the song "Simply Irresistible."

Apparently our performance wasn't.

When the music stopped, penalty flags were all over the field. Just as the show's promotions promised, we had gone from the thrill of victory to the agony of my two left feet.

"The tango did to you what no linebacker could do," said the first judge, Len Goodman. "It stopped you in your tracks."

"You lacked your usual charisma," added the next judge, Bruno Tonioli. "Apart from the technical flaws, you didn't shine as you usually do."

And the third judge, Carrie Ann Inaba, observed, "This wasn't your best dance."

The unimpressed judges awarded our team only 19 out of a possible 30 points, our worst performance up to that point. Afterward I assured Len, Bruno, and Carrie Ann that we would work harder and do better. I meant it too.

We had been practicing four hours a day. After the tango tripped me up, we cranked up our practices to six, seven, and eight hours a day. More important, I suggested an adjustment in *how* we practiced.

RISING TO THE OCCASION

Cheryl was too gracious to point out that, in the previous season, she and Drew Lachey had tangoed to a perfect 30 score. She didn't have to. It was humbling to admit it, but I knew that I was the problem on our team. Since I'm committed to doing whatever it takes to make the most of my opportunities, a change seemed in order. So I accepted responsibility and then devised a plan to become a better performer.

To make sure I mastered the rest of our routines—which required learning the paso doble, samba, jive disco, waltz, mambo, fox-trot, and rumba dances—I suggested to Cheryl that we stop practicing like dancers and approach each routine more like a football team learning new plays.

Cheryl had been teaching me our numbers the way she would teach a dancer, walking me through each routine as one fluid number. But I was accustomed to learning complex plays by breaking them down step-by-step and then practicing each segment over and over, mastering the techniques and moves through repetition before moving on to the next. My coaches had always broken plays down for us in that way.

I told Cheryl that once I had each segment of a dance routine down pat and stored in my muscle memory, then I could put it all together. Mastering a routine in that way would give me the confidence to relax and enjoy myself, which was critical for winning over the judges and audience.

Cheryl, to her credit, made the adjustment necessary to transform a running back into a dancing machine. She changed her teaching and training methods to suit my style of learning. And the rest is history. Cheryl and I came back to win the championship by defeating a great team who had mopped up in the tango: actor Mario Lopez and his partner, Karina Smirnoff.

More than twenty-seven million viewers watched our winning freestyle dance—and the response was almost overwhelming. Sure, I had to endure some teasing about the wardrobe they'd put me in over the course of the season—including silk vests, M. C. Hammer pants, and gold dance shoes. But our office was also flooded with new opportunities: offers for endorsements, commercials, television series, partnerships, and business deals of all kinds. My Q score, which advertising agencies and their clients use to measure factors such as likeability and recognition, had always been high, but it really soared after my appearance on the show.

Did I receive long-term benefits from the exposure that came with this opportunity? No doubt about it. But my success on *Dancing with the Stars* also benefited those who work for me in my current businesses and those who'll be on the payroll of my future ventures. Other beneficiaries include the young people who are served by our charitable foundation and its programs. (I'll tell you more about those in chapter 10.)

That's an important thing to remember when it comes to trying something new. When we make the most of opportunities that help us develop and multiply our blessings, others often reap rewards as well.

God wants us to keep stretching and growing throughout our time on this earth. I view opportunities as doors God opens to keep us moving down his chosen path. But we have to be careful. Sometimes opportunities come that are not from God and do not match up to our highest principles and long-term goals. Sometimes what looks like an opportunity is actually a sidetrack. So discernment is necessary—plus a lot of prayer.

Sometimes God may open a door that you hesitate to walk through. You may have many doubts. You may not see any reason to proceed. Yet when you step through it, your life changes in wonderful ways beyond anything you might have imagined.

That was what happened to me with *Dancing with the Stars*. I had thought it might be a fun competition that would help me stay in shape and maybe attract some endorsement deals. Yet being on that show helped me expand my territory beyond anything I could have imagined. I can't tell you how many times men have stopped me in restaurants or airports to tell me that their wives had no idea I was a professional football player but they had become fans from watching me on *Dancing with the Stars*.

My invitation to be a guest in one of the pilot episodes of *Who Do You Think You Are?* came as the result of my appearance on *DWTS*. And years after Cheryl and I won the championship, I still receive offers to appear in reality series, sitcoms, awards shows, and other productions. My reality-TV experiences have widened my horizons while I was doing something that my entire family—from our children to their cousins, aunts and uncles, and grandparents—has enjoyed together.

To tell you the truth, though, I'm a little worried that our youngest kids may grow up thinking that their daddy was just a TV dancer! Yeah, right—like I would let that happen. When they get older, I may require them to watch my Dallas Cowboys game films just to straighten them out.

OPEN DOORS AND CLOSED DOORS

Dancing with the Stars turned out to be a great opportunity for me, and I'm really glad I chose to walk through that door when it opened. The Lord guides us by both opening and closing doors along our journey through life, and there are opportunities in each. A closed door is often an invitation to step back and look harder or even take a different direction.

In those moments of my life when I encounter closed doors, I try to tell myself, "God brought you this far. He is not going to let you down." Then I step back and look beyond the problem to the opportunity that is being presented. Is this the time to set off in another direction? Or would it be wiser to wait, regroup, and move ahead at a later time?

I retired from football in 2005 fully prepared to do big things in commercial real estate. As it turned out, that wasn't the best time to be launching a career in that particular market. Between 2006 and 2009, real-estate developers and commercial and residential builders across the country struggled. Many went bankrupt or fled the business.

These developments didn't exactly slam the door on my plans to pursue a career in that field, but I did have to pull back and reassess. I've still kept my hand in while waiting for the market to revive, but I've also taken the opportunity to build up the construction side of my business, taking on small jobs to gain experience, establish a reputation, and develop clients. Meanwhile, I'm trying to take the long view when it comes to real estate. I believe the market will pick up eventually. But in the meantime, I'm doing all I can to prepare myself and to expand my horizons in other areas.

THE DANGERS OF SHORTSIGHTEDNESS

In difficult situations, many people lose faith, panic, and look for quick fixes. But in my view, that's exactly the kind of short-term mentality that contributed to the decline of the banking, mortgage, and financial markets. So many people were blinded by fast profits that they allowed the entire economic infrastructure to collapse and fail.

The same shortsightedness leads others to the latest diet pill and the daily lottery. In recent years even the sports arena has been plagued with accounts of professional athletes pumping up their bodies with steroids and other drugs rather than taking the time and making the effort to build strength through proper training. Sadly, many of those who went for the quick fix have suffered health problems from the side effects of the drugs or have seen their reputations tarnished or ruined—and all because they were shortsighted instead of farsighted.

This lack of a long-term vision can cripple our ability to fully develop our gifts and to seek God's blessing. In much the same way, selfishness and lack of empathy can prevent us from spotting the most important opportunity life presents us—the opportunity to bless others.

The parable of the Good Samaritan in the Gospel of Luke (10:30-37) tells of just such an opportunity that presented itself to two travelers on the road from Jerusalem to Jericho. A fellow Jew had been viciously attacked by thieves, stripped, and left half-dead on the roadside. But these two travelers were too busy and caught up in their own affairs to pay any attention, so they walked on and missed the opportunity to be a blessing—and to be blessed.

Next came a Samaritan, whose people were traditionally considered enemies of the Jews. He, too, saw the injured man. But unlike the previous travelers, the Samaritan took the opportunity to show compassion by helping the injured man. He treated his wounds with oil and wine, put him on his own donkey, and took him to an inn, where he cared for him. The next day, the Samaritan had to continue his own journey, but he left money with the innkeeper so that the injured man could stay until he had recovered.

I suppose the two travelers who saw the man bleeding on the roadside had their excuses for not stopping to help. So do we. We've all had times in our lives when we could have reached out and helped another human being but felt we had to move on. And we may have been right.

But we also may have missed an opportunity for blessing.

In this story, the man who showed mercy was a supposed enemy of the Jewish people, a despised foreigner, yet his willingness to take the opportunity to help showed that he was the true "neighbor" of the injured Jewish man.

Jesus held up the Good Samaritan as an example, telling his followers to "go and do the same" (verse 37, NLT). God wants us to take every possible opportunity to help not only those we think of as our neighbors, but anyone in need.

Sometimes they might benefit from just a kind word or a helping hand. Other times we, like the Good Samaritan, might have to reach into our pockets. But unless we prepare ourselves for these opportunities, we may fail to see them or take advantage of them. We may find that we're too busy or too distracted even to see the opportunity that is right in front of our noses—the opportunity that God wants to use to change our lives.

CHAPTER 7
BUILD YOUR TEAM

As iron sharpens iron,
so one person sharpens another.

PROVERBS 27:17

"Moooooose! Mooooooose!"

For me, that will always be the song of teamwork.

Our Cowboys fullback, Daryl Johnston, was such an unselfish team player that even opposing fans would call out his nickname to show their appreciation for his dedication and commitment. *Mooooooose* will always be music to my ears, and I have a film clip to go with it. That chant and these memories stream through my mind whenever I think of Daryl and the example he set.

I see Moose in the huddle during a game. He's telling me that there is a defender who is too big and strong for him to block squared up on the next running play. "I have to cut him at the ankle, and I'm going to cut his outside leg," he says.

In the next scene I'm running with the ball, and Moose does just what he promised. He dives low at the linebacker's outside leg, and his neck snaps back as he hits the defender and topples him like a lumberjack taking down a huge tree.

Daylight appears in the defense, and I run for it.

There is one final segment in my memory's highlight film of this special teammate. In it, I see Daryl on the sidelines looking woozy as the trainers give him smelling salts. He takes a deep whiff, rubs his neck, straightens his back, snaps his helmet strap in place, and jogs back onto the field with the fans yelling, "Moooooose! Moooooose!"

Now you know why my emotions ran so high when I thanked Daryl Johnston in my induction speech on August 7, 2010. I may go down as one of the biggest stage hogs in the history of the Hall of Fame, but that doesn't bother me. There were so many people responsible for lifting me up and putting me on that platform. And I was not leaving without thanking as many of them as I could. Because without teammates like Moose, there's no way I could have accomplished anything.

THE IMPORTANCE OF TEAMWORK

A football team wins championships when players put their individual interests aside and direct all their efforts to achieving the goals of the team. The same holds true in any human endeavor. We can build rocket ships, cities of skyscrapers, and global corporations only because thousands of individuals agree to share information, solve problems, and labor together. In recent years, scientists have concluded that even more than brainpower, it is the willingness of individuals to put aside their personal interests to serve the needs of a group that "lies at the root of human achievement," according to a *New York Times* report.

The same report noted that in most other species, only close relatives are known to work together and to help each other. Our ability to form large social networks—teams—allows us to learn from each other, innovate, and accomplish more than any other species. Of course, close human relatives benefit from doing the same thing. Human families thrive when husbands and wives, parents and children, grandparents and other relations choose to set aside their personal agendas and work together.

I'm concerned about the state of teamwork in our country. We've become so polarized politically and financially that we seem to have forgotten we are all in this together. We need to work together and to look out for one another. Democrat and Republican, rich and poor, minority and majority, we are all citizens of this nation and inhabitants of this planet. Sometimes we have to make sacrifices

I'm concerned about the state of teamwork in our country. We've become so polarized politically and financially that we seem to have forgotten we are all in this together. We need to work together and to look out for one another. Democrat and Republican, rich and poor, minority and majority, we are all citizens of this nation and inhabitants of this planet. Sometimes we have to make sacrifices together so that we can all live and thrive together. I believe that all of us, including our elected officials, need to be better teammates.

together so that we can all live and thrive together. I believe that all of us, including our elected officials, need to be better teammates, to work together to serve our highest purpose, and to make the most of our time on this earth while preparing for what awaits us in the next life.

My football teammates and I each had our own positions and responsibilities, but we shared common goals. We could not have accomplished those goals without each other. We worked together. We supported one another. We lifted each other up. When one of us was hurt or in trouble, we went to his aid. We communicated with each other by listening as well as talking. And if one of us slacked off as a teammate in practice and especially in a game, we'd hear about it immediately. Our coaches and fellow players let us know that we needed to pick it up and get moving.

Part of that close teamwork grows out of the fact that the members of a college or professional football team live together night and day for much of their playing careers. In the preseason and on road trips, they sleep and eat and play together. Bonds are formed. Respect and trust are established.

Many times I see those elements lacking in the real world. Maybe that's why teamwork seems so hard. Many people don't put in as much as they try to take out of friendships and relationships. They don't take the time to form bonds, to establish mutual trust and respect, or to communicate honestly. That doesn't make teamwork less important, though. It just makes it a little more challenging.

Now that I've been out of football for a few years, I've noticed that many people don't have a very good grasp of their responsibilities as teammates, whether it's in their friendships, business relationships, or even their families. On a football team, if a player decides that he is bigger than the team and more important than his fellow players, they set him straight. You just don't get away with it for long. The feedback may come in the form of a slap to the side of your helmet.

The members of your life team may not communicate as clearly or call you out as readily as the members of my football team did. So you have to be more self-aware, more in tune with the needs of your friends, and more sensitive about how you treat them and what you demand of them.

Friends and coworkers may not give you the same feedback as teammates when you let them down. Instead, they may just walk away or write you off. Even family might hold back from letting you know that you're not pulling your weight. So you need to be aware that your success and that of your team requires your full cooperation and mutual support.

THE E-TEAM

My Lord and Savior is the most important figure in my life. Everything I am and every fiber of my being belongs to him. He has been my rock and my Savior, and whatever I have accomplished is due to his presence in my life. My life goes so much better when I realize that, yes, we're teammates—but it's his team, not mine.

I have also been blessed to have many angels here on earth—people I think of as my "E-team." This group is not limited to those who've stood with me on the football field. So many people have encouraged and supported me. Sometimes they've lifted me up by challenging and confronting me. Every now and then, they've dared me to enlarge my territory even beyond what I'd dreamed myself.

Those who've enlightened and elevated me include my wife, my parents, my grandparents, and other family members, as well as my coaches, teachers, fellow athletes, pastors, sports agents, and many others. I acknowledged and thanked many of them in my Hall of Fame speech, and my words for each of them were from the heart.

My thanks to Daryl Johnston, in particular, seemed to touch many people in a special way. Maybe that's because so many people have had someone who helped them succeed and maybe they've never had the opportunity to thank that person publicly. So in a sense I spoke for many people that day when I recognized and thanked a team member whose presence in my life made me better and whose dedication and commitment inspired me too.

"Daryl Johnston, where are you? Will you please stand? You mean the world to me, not just because we shared the same back-field, but also because you sacrificed so much for me. People don't understand what it took to be a fullback in our system, the sacrifices you made not simply with your body but your whole spirit. You took care of me as though you were taking care of your little brother. Without you, I know today would not have been possible. I love you from the bottom of my heart."

Then, once again, came the chant: "Moooooose! Moooooose!"

Daryl was drafted by Dallas in 1989, a year before I joined the team. He became the most respected fullback in the league—the first NFL fullback invited to the Pro Bowl—but had to retire after eleven years. Chronic neck injuries, including two herniated disks, made it impossible for him to keep playing.

I'm sure you can imagine how much I missed him—not just his blocking, but his spirit, too. Moose inspired me on the field and in practice, sure, but his impact on me went well beyond the mutual respect players often share.

Throughout his career in the NFL, Moose led the league in unselfishness and courage. He was a 230- to 240-pound guy who had to take on bigger and stronger linebackers nearly every play. I've mentioned that the Cowboys' strategy during most of my career was to keep hammering away with the same play, the lead draw. The main blocker on that play was almost always Daryl Johnston.

On the lead draw, Moose was positioned five yards behind the line of scrimmage prior to the snap. When the ball was hiked, I shuffled a step to get the handoff from the quarterback, and Daryl had to take on the opposing linebacker as he came charging in with a full head of steam. Usually they clashed in a head-on, full-body collision that was absorbed by Daryl's head, neck, and shoulders.

My teammate was often overmatched physically, but my record-breaking rushing yardage and our three shared Super Bowl victories serve as testimony that Daryl usually found a way to keep the defender from reaching me. Fans watching in the stands or on television might have noticed the great blocker who opened running room for me. Even so, I don't think most of them gave much thought to the punishment Daryl took while doing that.

I did. Some nights after games, my mind would flash images of Moose hitting and being hit with such force that I wondered how he ever pulled himself up off the field. Even more disturbing were the sounds of those collisions. Honestly, the crack of helmets and pads and body parts smashing into each other was so loud it was like running through a ten-car pileup. Every play.

I often wondered how long his body could take the punishment. I'm sure he thought the same thing about me as well. As much as I appreciated him and all he did for our team and for me, I worried about his health then and still do.

I think of Moose whenever I see the movie *In the Line of Fire*, in which Clint Eastwood plays a Secret Service agent who takes a bullet for the president. Moose took so many bullets for me. I was sorry to see his career end prematurely, but I was also relieved that he left before his neck injury caused him even greater problems.

Like many football players, Daryl worried that the head blows and concussions he experienced on the field might endanger his physical and mental health later in life. So he was relieved with the results of a recent brain study that found his brain scans were "remarkably clear."

Today Moose looks great. And now, instead of blocking, he talks. He is a member of the Fox Sports broadcasting team, and I hope he has a long and successful career there. Daryl is still giving selflessly in the community, too, whether it's working with Special Olympics, the Children's Cancer Fund, Cystic Fibrosis Foundation, literacy programs, or other good causes.

You might have noticed I'm a dedicated Daryl Johnston fan. And I'm afraid he will have to put up with one recurring problem:

I plan to continue thanking him publicly and loudly for the rest of our lives. I'm doing another tribute to Moose in this book because he is the ultimate example of a selfless teammate on the football field. He played with such passion and dedication that he was cheered in stadiums around the league. Believe me, that didn't happen to many Cowboys back when we were beating so many teams.

I would also like to state for the record that I also blocked for Moose from time to time, including once in my rookie year when I threw a block on a draw play that allowed him to score a touchdown on a 12-yard run!

You're welcome, Moose.

THE MEANING OF A TEAM

In John 15:13, Jesus describes a true friend: "Greater love hath no man than this, that a man lay down his life for his friends" (KJV). That's a great picture of unselfish teamwork—as long as we keep it in perspective.

Certainly football is a tough sport. Physical injury and pain are part of the game. It's not unusual for us football players to think of ourselves as warriors. But our form of combat is nothing like that experienced by true warriors. So let me acknowledge that every day American military troops in Afghanistan, Iraq, and around the world make the ultimate sacrifice on behalf of our country and freedom, and for their fellow men and women in the service.

They are bona fide heroes. Their sacrifices on the battlefield are on a scale far beyond anything Moose and I ever experienced on the playing field. I respect and honor them, as well as those who give so much in humanitarian and philanthropic efforts around the world, whether they are doctors, nurses, missionaries, firefighters, police officers, or volunteers for charitable organizations. Many are literally laying down their lives for others.

That's not true of most of us, though. The chances that we will be asked to actually die for another person are slim. And I can't imagine many circumstances in which I would want someone to die for me. But we do choose every day whether to look after our own selfish interests first or put someone else ahead of those interests. Choosing to sacrifice our own needs for the needs of others or for the sake of the larger group—that's the real meaning of love and teamwork.

I benefited greatly from parents who put the interests of all their children above their own. I also had teachers, coaches, and teammates who cared enough to cheer my victories, console me in defeat, and set me straight when I needed to hear the truth, even if I didn't like it. Such friends are rare, and I am grateful for them. I do all I can to be as good a friend to them as they have been to me.

Most of us are born self-centered because we come into this world with limited awareness. As newborns and toddlers and often even as teenagers, we tend to think the universe revolves around our needs. Empathy, the ability to put ourselves in the shoes of other people, comes with maturity. Only after we've experienced the world beyond our backyards do we begin to understand how much we all depend on each other.

We might all remain as self-centered as children if our survival and success as adults did not require cooperation and social networks. And by "social network" I'm not just referring to Facebook. Sports teams, business teams, prayer teams, service organizations, neighborhoods, communities, states, and nations are all examples of social networks. Certain levels of mutual trust and cooperation must be maintained in all of those networks. Otherwise there would be no order. Chaos would rule.

There is yet another important aspect of teamwork in our daily lives. We need each other not only to maintain order, but to grow and flourish. Proverbs 27:17 reminds us,

> *As iron sharpens iron,*
> *so one person sharpens another.*

The people around you must make you better and make you want to be better—and you must do the same for them. Someone who brings out less than your best is not a good teammate or a true friend.

We've all had friends who may have once been uplifting and inspiring people but have drifted downward. You don't want them taking you down too. Sometimes you will have to cut ties with friends who become liabilities. Do your best to set them on a better course. Give them a chance to find their way back. But if they aren't willing to do what it takes or to listen to your advice, walk away. Make the break with care and consideration. Let them know you will always value them, but do not put your dreams at risk because they have lost sight of theirs.

Amos 3:3 offers another basic truth of friendship. This passage asks, "Can two walk together, except they be agreed?" (KJV). True teammates have similar goals and dreams. That doesn't mean friends will always see eye to eye. Sometimes it takes a true friend to give you a reality check, or at least to tell you that there is a piece of lettuce stuck on your tooth! But true friends do agree on long-term goals and fundamental principles. They support each other. They also believe that there is enough success out there for both of them—enough pieces of the pie for everyone.

The strength of your friendships depends on the strength of the bonds you create. To have a friend, you must be a friend. If you are not willing to make sacrifices for others and celebrate their accomplishments with them, you can't expect that they'll be there for you.

The simple fact is that we need each other, and all of us need people in our lives who are supportive and encouraging. This is the next necessary element in achieving your purpose in life.

Your dreams and goals set the vision, purpose, and path for your life. Sticking to the principles you value creates strength of character, which gives you the courage to deal with your fears and the commitment to carry on despite challenges. Opportunities are the doorways you walk through to find God's plan for your life. But it is your personal team—those who are bound together in love, loyalty, and shared purpose—that makes it possible for you to become your best and enjoy the outcome.

SPEECH TEAM

When the time came for me to be inducted into the Pro Football Hall of Fame, I wanted to take the opportunity to express my gratitude to all of my football, business, and personal team members. I also wanted to deliver a speech that would inspire and motivate others to live their dreams. I was determined to deliver the best speech I had ever given, one that represented my best effort, the effort of a champion not just in sports but also in life. To accomplish those goals, I had to face a personal challenge that I haven't talked about publicly.

I had to deal with my "Emmitt-isms."

My brain sometimes whirls faster than I can speak, and as a result I've been known to mess up, spilling out the wrong words or made-up words or falling into slang and shortcut words that aren't exactly the King's English. I've been teased and criticized for this—relentlessly in some quarters—so I've tried to work on it.

I first became self-conscious about speaking properly when I tried my hand at sports broadcasting. The folks at the NFL network offered to help by introducing me to someone who has become a very important member of my team.

Former USC theater professor Arthur Samuel Joseph is a speech coach extraordinaire whose Vocal Awareness method has helped thousands of actors, athletes, singers, broadcasters, politicians, and business leaders over the course of his forty-year career. I've worked with Arthur off and on over the last five years or so. And when I was selected for the Hall of Fame, I asked him to help me prepare for the landmark moment in my life.

If you've seen the movie *The King's Speech*, you have only a hint of what Arthur and I went through. We began working on the speech and my delivery in March and continued for four months either in person or on the phone. The original speech was twenty-five minutes long, and we put in more than one hundred hours together. I worked another one hundred hours on my own—memorizing, reciting, videotaping, reviewing, and doing my best to master every word, every emotion, every pause and inflection.

Poor Pat. My wife had to listen to that speech day and night for months. I'm sure she knew it better than I did because I'd lie in bed reciting it line by line while she slept—or tried to sleep. Come to think of it, our youngest child, Elijah Alexander James, probably knows the speech too. He was right there with us, preparing for his own big moment—his birth.

I followed the same basic training approach for that speech that I'd followed preparing for NFL games and *Dancing with the Stars*. I broke the speech into smaller segments and mastered it a little at a time. The goal was the same as playing football or dancing. I worked to master the playbook or the steps in the dance to the point where I was free to move without thinking. That way I could be as aggressive and creative as I wanted to be during the game or the performance.

Anytime the spotlight hits me, I don't want to be worrying or even thinking. I want to be loose, have fun, and enjoy the moment. I worked and worked at memorizing that speech so I would be free to stand up there and speak without wrangling paper, racking my brain to remember the content, or worrying I'd commit an Emmitt-ism. I was determined to speak with all the power, emotion, and clarity I could muster. I wanted to have that speech out of my head and in my heart.

Arthur's job was to sharpen my delivery, and yes, he had his work cut out for him. Fortunately, my speech coach is a master whose talents go beyond the voice and into the soul. He has a finely tuned sixth sense for the emotions conveyed by each person's voice, and he's very effective at teaching vocal awareness and helping clients deliver a speech with body, mind, and spirit. One of his main challenges was slowing me down. I tend to speak faster and faster as my emotions heat up, and I knew this would be a very emotional speech. So I worked with Arthur to slow the pace of my delivery so that I gave myself time to breathe, allowing the words to flow naturally.

Controlling my emotions during that speech would be another challenge. I wrote it from the heart, and the audience would include nearly all of the most important people in my life, so I knew there was a chance I would lose it at the podium. During those four months of practicing the speech, in fact, I was a serial crybaby. I'd think about all of my family and friends and teammates and coaches in the audience and all that they meant to me, and man, oh man . . . my eyes welled up nearly every time I practiced it. Arthur did the same when he heard it. We were a mess. But we were also a team, and we developed strategies together to help me hold it together on the big day.

A last-minute challenge came when we were told to cut three minutes from the speech. By then the whole piece was etched in my brain like words in granite, so cutting and pasting and rearranging the contents, then rememorizing the revised speech at that late date, was a real challenge.

By the way, this explains the "lost" part of my original speech. In our scramble to revise, we accidentally cut out references to my alma mater, the University of Florida. This was especially embarrassing because the Gators' current coach, Urban Meyer, and several others from my school were in the audience. I've asked for their forgiveness, and I think they've given it to me. (Go, Gators!)

Arthur and I were still working on the speech revisions just minutes before the ceremony—and, to be honest, having a really, really hard time getting it right. I kept messing up time after time, which only made me more nervous. I was not alone. Later, Pat said she was so tense watching me that she was afraid she might give birth right then and there! (Elijah wasn't in any hurry, as it turned out. He was born six and a half weeks later, on September 22.)

It's a good thing that Arthur and I had prepared so well, because when the time came for me to take the stage with the others, I was all over the place. But then his training kicked in, and I told myself to stop trying and focus on enjoying the moment. *Forget it—whatever comes out, comes out.*

In the days leading up to the ceremony, I'd talked with several former players who were already in the Hall of Fame, and they all had advised me to be sure to enjoy the moment. "This will be one of the highlights of your life, so be sure to take it all in," they'd said. "Don't rush through it. Bask in the accomplishment. You've earned this."

I appreciated their encouraging words, and I remembered that nugget of advice as I gathered with my fellow inductees—Jerry Rice, John Randle, Russ Grimm, Rickey Jackson, Floyd Little, and Dick LeBeau—all of whom were taking bets on which of us would be the first to cry.

"Go ahead and bet on me," I told them. "I'll lose it for sure. I know it'll happen."

Jerry spoke before I did and broke the dike, so that's one thing I didn't have to worry about. I was the last to speak, and when I stepped up and started into the speech, I first thanked the source: "my Lord and Savior Jesus Christ." Then I took a deep, calming breath.

From that point forward, it was "Game *on!*" As you may have seen—or can still see on YouTube.com and other Internet sites— my emotions were definitely engaged, but Arthur's coaching, many hours of practice, and more than a few deep breaths kept me in the game. Even when I lost my way a little in the middle of the speech, Arthur had built in a mental catch-up place so I could compose myself and get back in sync with what he calls "conscious awareness." I jumped back into the groove as I thanked my parents, coaches, family, and teammates that day. I loved it, but darn near lost it when the fans in the audience sensed who was coming up next on my list and began chanting "Moooooose!"

I had a chance in that speech to thank just about every teammate who had helped me get to that moment. But I didn't have a chance to thank the one member of my team who helped me actually deliver the speech—Arthur himself. He was too modest to write it into the speech. So I'll thank him now.

Thanks, Coach Arthur. You're the greatest!

THE TEAM MAKES THE DIFFERENCE

No one makes it alone in this world.

The team of supporters, advisers, and encouragers you put together helps determine just how far you will travel here on earth.

As the song says, "we all need somebody to lean on." More important, we need someone we can count on not just to support and encourage us, but also to keep us on the path of our dreams and God's plan for our lives.

If you have one or two people in your life willing to step up, put their hands on your shoulders, and turn you around when you are lost, then you are truly blessed. I was fortunate to have responsible and caring people willing to set me straight. One of those people was my high-school coach, Dwight Thomas. He was a great coach but an even better teacher, and he refused to let me get away with giving less than my best.

Early in my high-school career, a reporter was interviewing me just before practice one day, and I got a little carried away talking about myself. Coach Thomas listened in without comment as I told the newspaper reporter how I was able to do this and that in the previous game. I made the mistake of not mentioning that my teammates had made it possible for me to fulfill my role on the field by giving me the ball and blocking for me.

Coach Thomas didn't say a word at the time. But later, during a scrimmage, he set me straight with a simple but effective lesson. When I wasn't around, he instructed the offensive line not to block for me on a play we were running against our defense. We were in full pads, so there was no holding back.

The quarterback handed me the ball. I took one step, and the entire defense steamrollered me. I was like one of those cartoon characters that you have to peel off the ground with a spatula. It was a humbling experience to see how little my press clippings and my athletic ability mattered when no one was blocking for me.

Our offensive line watched and laughed as I struggled to my feet and returned to the huddle. In that moment, I became a new teammate. I never again talked to a reporter, or anyone, about my performance in a game without giving due credit to my teammates and coaches.

HELPING EACH OTHER UP

Coach Thomas did me a big favor, and he added another supportive plank to the foundation of my character by making it clear that I was part of a team, and without my teammates, I wasn't going anywhere. Neither are you.

Without family members, coaches, teachers, classmates, coworkers, and friends who want you to succeed, the odds are stacked against you. The more people you have on your team who are willing to buy into your dreams, the more opportunities you will have and the higher you will climb. If you try to make it on your own, you will have a very difficult journey.

That simple truth has existed since men and women have walked this earth. Ecclesiastes 4:9-10 cautions about this:

> *Two are better than one,*
> *because they have a good return for their labor:*
> *If either of them falls down,*
> *one can help the other up.*
> *But pity anyone who falls*
> *and has no one to help them up.*

Now might be the time to ask yourself, "Who would reach out to me if I fell?" If you can't think of anyone, look for ways to mend lost connections or to nurture new ones. If you can identify even a small number of people whom you can truly count on, consider yourself blessed. But don't make the mistake of taking them for granted, even if they are family members. I recommend that, at least a couple of times a year, you go to the members of your support team and ask how you can be a better friend to each of them.

And don't just ask—listen to the answer. Pay attention. Try to *be* the kind of friend, family member, teammate, or colleague you would want to have supporting you.

INVESTING IN RELATIONSHIPS

A wise mother once said to me that she patiently listens to her children even when they jabber about inconsequential matters "because if I keep the lines of communication open, they will still come to me when they are older and have really important things to talk about." That mother was investing in her relationship with her children.

You cannot take money out of an IRA unless you put money into it. The same holds true with relationships, especially those you depend on the most. You cannot continually make withdrawals from a friendship without making deposits, too. You can't ask a friend to do for you what you refuse to do for him or her. If you're not there when your friends need you, how can you expect them to be there for you?

Have you ever had someone you hardly know hit you up for a loan or ask to borrow your car? Some people just don't understand that the bigger the withdrawal you hope to make, the greater the deposit required.

I don't mean we should give to our friends just so that they will give back to us or that we should keep strict accounts to be sure we're not giving more than anyone else. Most relationships feature a certain give and take. Sometimes you give more than you receive, and sometimes you receive more than you can give at the time.

Over the long haul, however, the model for being a good teammate, good friend, or good partner is that of mutual support. It flows both ways. Yet so many people seem to have a friendship model that runs more like a one-way street. We've all had friends who drain us by constantly dumping their problems on us, but just aren't around when we have problems of our own. Such an "overdrawn" friendship account just can't stay open for very long.

Investing in your relationships means treating your friends, colleagues, and teammates with respect. Be grateful for their presence in your life. Make sure they're aware of that gratitude. And be sure to make frequent "deposits" by giving as well as taking.

If you feel the need to "vent" to a friend, for instance, make sure that you have been willing to listen to that person in his or her down times too. And even then, be cautious. Most people have a limited capacity for listening to complaints and whining—especially whining. It's one thing to ask for advice and a friend's perspective when you are facing a challenge. It's another thing altogether to simply unload your anger and frustration on an innocent bystander.

To have even one person who wants the best for you is a blessing. If you have a friend like that on your team, take care of that relationship as you would a priceless gift—because that's exactly what it is.

NOT ALL FRIENDS ARE EQUAL

You will have many people come through your life. Many of them will have a positive impact, and some will join the ranks of your trusted teammates. But as you build a team of those you trust to have your best interests at heart, you need to understand that not all relationships are equal. Some people will buy into your success without reservation, while others may have their own agendas or concerns. Some may simply be too busy. Others may be jealous or even hateful. A few may wish you harm. Even someone you like and who wishes you well may not be someone you can trust with your secrets, your dreams and desires, or your fears.

That's life. Not everyone will want to be a dedicated and committed member of your team or have you on their team. Not everyone *needs* to be on your team. The key is to understand what kind of friends you have and be careful about who you trust with what part of your life.

How can you tell? Bishop Jakes of Potter's House church, whom I consider a friend and an important member of my team, has some helpful advice about this. He suggests that there are three types of friends, and only one kind is to be trusted with your dreams if you hope to achieve your God-given destiny. The three kinds of friends are

- comrades,
- constituents, and
- confidants.

Comrades for the Battle

Your comrades are your casual friends and temporary teammates. They don't really invest much time or effort in the relationship, but for some period they are willing to stand with you against a common enemy or opponent. You join forces and work together only because of that shared concern, and usually for a limited period of time.

Comrades may be people you team up with for a time-limited political battle—an issue at your children's school, for instance. Because you'll only be together for a while, you don't invest a lot of energy or trust in developing these relationships. That's not to say you can't be friendly with your comrades or enjoy their company. But it's good to be careful about demanding more of a relationship than is appropriate for the situation.

A good example of this kind of relationship is the kind I enjoyed with my Pro Bowl teammates. I loved playing alongside many of my former rivals in eight Pro Bowl games. For Pro Bowls, the two opposing teams are made up of those players judged the best across the entire NFL. For that one game, players from competing teams become teammates.

I always had fun playing alongside these former rivals. We had all been selected by a vote of our peers, so I felt honored to be there, playing with the best in each division. Most of my fellow Pro Bowl players were great guys, and we got along pretty well.

But we were always guarded in what we said about ourselves, our teams, and our coaches.

I wasn't about to hand any of my Pro Bowl teammates the Cowboys' playbook, for instance, nor would I have confided in them about a nagging injury or a weakness in the Dallas defense. They wouldn't confide such things to me, either. We had more limited loyalty to each other than they did to the teammates who worked and played with them in the regular season.

We did watch out for each other, though, especially when it came to avoiding injury. That's a number one priority for nearly everybody—to have fun, not to get hurt, and not to hurt anyone else. After all, the Pro Bowl is really just an exhibition game, and nobody wants to risk his health and his career for an exhibition.

The only time the Pro Bowl game may become as physical as a regular season game is if the score is close near the end of the game. In that situation, each player begins thinking about the bonus money that goes to those on the winning team—which in my day was between $1,500 and $2,500. With that money on the line while the clock is ticking down, you might see a little more intensity out there.

My relationship with my Pro Bowl colleagues was typical of a comrade-type friendship. And there's absolutely nothing wrong with having comrades. In fact, many of the people you interact with each day may qualify for this category of friendship. Your comrades can be a nice source of company and wonderful allies in whatever battle you are fighting together. But because this kind of relationship tends to be narrowly focused and time limited, you would be wise not to overshare or to expect too much of your comrades outside your chosen arena.

Your Constituents

The same is true of *constituents*, who become teammates with you for the opposite reason of comrades. Instead of sharing an enemy, they share a belief with you. I heard a wise man say, "They are not into you. They are into what you are for."

Constituents will walk with you only as long as you can help them further their agenda. If they find someone who takes them farther or faster in pursuit of that goal, they may well abandon you. Constituents can be fly-by-night friends or social climbers who see you as a means to an end. Once you have served or out- lived that purpose, it's "so long, Charlie."

In most cases, NFL players view their team owners and execu- tives as constituents. These management representatives recruit, draft, and trade players based on the value they place on the players' talents and the contributions they believe the players can make to the team. Team owners share with their players the desire to win the Super Bowl. But if a player gets injured or doesn't perform to expectations, the team owner and his execu- tives will replace him.

Your boss or employer and even your coworkers are likely to be constituents, whose friendship with you is based on the goals you share at work. That relationship can serve the needs of both parties as long as you show the same commitment to those goals. But it's vital to keep in mind that their loyalty is not to you as a person, but to what you represent and how you can help them.

Again, there is nothing wrong with that, as long as you remember that both of these kinds of friendships are limited. You may well enjoy your interaction with your constituents. But your gut often will tell you that neither comrades nor constituents are to be trusted with your innermost feelings, hopes, or fears. In unguarded moments you might be tempted to confide in them as if your bond were stronger, but you may live to regret it. Both comrades and constituents might betray you to advance their own agendas or to give themselves an advantage. You can count on the fact that most of them will put their own interests ahead of yours. That's just human nature, and it's understandable.

Confidants You Can Count On

Far more rare—except on the football field where the team concept rules—are those willing to put their own best interests on hold for you. How many people do you know who are willing to always celebrate your victories with you and console and encourage you in hard times? How many are truly happy for your successes or sincerely sad when you are down?

You may find it easier to list the people who feel depressed or cheated when you find success or those who secretly enjoy it when you stumble or fail. That, too, is human nature, I'm afraid. Not all people are like that, of course, but there are far more comrades and constituents in everyone's life than there are *confidants*.

Confidants are those people who love and support you unconditionally. They are the best teammates you'll find because they are there for you in good times and in bad. As a professional athlete, I met many people who wanted to be my friend when I was playing well, earning a great salary, and making the fans happy. I was glad for their presence in my life, but I realized that there were limits to our relationship.

You will meet very few people who can be trusted as confidants. Mostly, my confidants, and yours too, are drawn from family, spouses, and other loved ones. Or they might be those people who were loyal friends long before you had anything of value that they might covet.

TEAM ASSESSMENT

This is tricky territory, because as you journey through life, achieve your goals, and live your dreams, some of your initial confidants may prove to no longer be worthy of your highest levels of trust. Their love may come with conditions that make them no longer trustworthy. My mother was addressing this fact when she cautioned me that "not everybody can go where you go." (Pat says the same thing to me now.)

My mother was warning me that people and circumstances change. Someone who once pushed you forward might eventually hold you back. You may outgrow some friends. Others may outgrow you. So it's a good idea to regularly assess your team of supporters and advisers and make sure they are still positive influences.

Understand also that even though you may be strong enough not to be negatively influenced by a friend who has taken on bad habits or fallen into bad behavior, the misdeeds of those around you can reflect badly on you and your reputation. The Bible says in 1 Corinthians 15:33, "Do not be misled: 'Bad company corrupts good character.'"

You would be wise to weed out those friends or teammates whose principles and values may no longer be in alignment with yours. Bishop Jakes offers similar advice when he says that we must not feed those who cannot feed us. He's not saying we shouldn't look out for the poor or feed the hungry! He's talking about your closest friends and confidants—your team. You want to surround yourself with an inner circle of people who will make you better and stronger, not drag you down.

I still share my dreams with many of my earliest confidants, especially my parents and other family members. But some of my old friends are no longer in that inner circle. Our relationship has changed, and that's okay. Most of them are still friends. I just don't share my greatest hopes and fears with them anymore.

Like selflessness, unconditional love is a rare and precious commodity, and that's what marks your true confidants. You can't expect to have many confidants of this caliber, but you can certainly do your best to nurture and appreciate those who come your way.

My wife, Pat, and our children have multiplied my blessings when it comes to unconditional love. My wife is a beautiful woman, but that is not what I value most about her. Pat is wise in ways that are difficult to fathom, and I lean on her for wisdom and perspective. Best of all, I share with her my grandest dreams, my most exciting thoughts, and also my deepest fears.

My wife may not be made of iron, but she sharpens me nonetheless. She doesn't just make me be a better man; she makes me *want to be* a better man. My wife is smarter than me by far, although someone recently pointed out that if she married me, maybe she's not all *that* smart!

Ideally, your team members have talents that mesh with yours, interests that match up with yours, and strengths that shore up your weaknesses. I'm grateful that Pat and I balance each other out in this way. We have a partnership that requires collaborative effort between us.

For example, I am not a details person when it comes to household affairs. At work, I hone in and cross every *t* and dot every *i*. At home, though, I let Pat handle the details because she is very good at organizing our activities with the kids and our social calendar, not to mention her own business. I can focus on business because I know she has the home front covered.

I also lean heavily on Pat when it comes to business advice. Like most women, she has a sixth sense when it comes to reading people and situations. I'm a firm believer that all men should pay close attention to that sixth sense.

In so many ways, my wife is an invaluable partner. But even better is the fact that she is such a deep well of unconditional love. Before I married her, I had a house. Now I have a home, and I am not embarrassed to tell people that it is filled with love. She and our children have created my dream life. We will always be there for each other.

Can you say the same about your most valued teammates in life? I suggest you look at those who fit that description for you and ask yourself, "If my life turned upside down, would they be there to help me turn it right side up? And if their lives turned upside down, would I be willing to stick around and walk them through that?"

If the answer is yes, count your blessings. If you aren't so sure, you might want to look again at those relationships. And you might want to ask if you've done all you can to deserve the unconditional love of others. The first requirement is that you love them unconditionally too.

I also have spiritual confidants, those people who help me on my spiritual journey. T. D. Jakes certainly stands at the head of this class. Bishop Jakes is another awesome sounding board I can reach out to, one of my most trusted confidants in spiritual, business, and personal matters. He is my spiritual father, a great communicator, and a brilliant businessman, too, so he's a triple-threat teammate.

Like my wife, Bishop Jakes can always be counted on to offer a fresh and deep perspective. I call him occasionally before going ahead with a business deal or making a move within my own businesses. He's also one of my favorite people to talk with about movies because his viewpoints are always surprising and his mind so far ranging. Bishop Jakes is very deep, and that depth makes him a compelling speaker and storyteller. His messages are like food to my soul.

Our relationship has shifted some since I first joined Potter's House because I have matured. In fact, Bishop Jakes and I are closer than ever before because he sometimes seeks my counsel now too. We have a lot in common because we both came from humble beginnings and then found ourselves thrust into the spotlight. While we are both grateful for all the support we've received, neither of us was prepared for all that attention. It's a little scary to realize that every person in the room has the ability to take photos or video of you and post it on the Internet where millions can see it. Anything you do and say can spread around the world in minutes, and that can be intimidating. Bishop Jakes and I both know what that's like, and that common ground has bolstered our friendship.

Your most trusted life teammates, your confidants, are those you trust to share your hopes and fears . . . and who share their hopes and fears with you as well. They're not there just for you. You're there for them too. You must be willing to listen openly and offer your honest advice to them if you hope for them to do the same for you. We all need people who believe in our destinies and stand ready to support and guide us so that we can fulfill God's plan for us.

PEOPLE WHO MAKE YOUR DREAMS COME TRUE

The teams in your life will come together in a variety of ways.

Some come to you by chance—or more likely, by God's choice. You're born into a certain family, for instance. You meet someone at school or at church or at work, hit it off, and end up becoming friends. Or you go on a blind date with a person you later end up marrying.

Some teams—like a football team or a military unit—may be put together by someone else, but the bonds forged by working together, playing together, and working for a common goal can be powerful.

Some relationships you seek out deliberately. Some seek you out. Some, like a marriage or a spiritual friendship, may develop when you reach a certain level of maturity and you're ready to take the next step.

All of these team relationships can be important, and some can be life changing. But if you are a leader in business or another arena, there's a special kind of team you need to be aware of—the team you choose to help you fulfill your purpose.

While on spring vacation to Hawaii with Pat and the kids a few years ago, I struck up a conversation with another dad who was on the beach with his family. After we'd talked about the weather and our kids and sports, he mentioned that he was in the construction business. We were staying at a very nice resort, and he seemed like a successful guy. I told him of my interest in real-estate development and construction, and I asked him what he thought were the keys to success in that field.

"I hired people who could make my dreams come true," he said.

I knew I liked this guy. He was being humble and honest. And his advice was very good. He said that you have to know your strengths and your weaknesses, and then you can hire people whose skill sets complement yours. The idea is to fit all the pieces together into a whole that is stronger than the individual parts.

As a businessman, I have worked very hard to do just that—to put together a team of people whom I respect and trust and whose skills and knowledge will help me take my enterprises farther than I might take them on my own. If I hope to enlarge my territory by creating and capitalizing on opportunities, my businesses need the proper infrastructure, including the right people in the right jobs.

When you put a business team together, you begin the process by acknowledging the areas where you need expertise. It's very critical that you know what you don't know. Nobody can know it all or do it all, so it's okay to admit that you can't either. I believe that the best thing I can do to build a legacy is to have a team around me that shares my dreams and can work with me to make them happen.

Of course, once you put a team together, you have to listen to your team members and let them do their jobs. Some people—yes, sometimes even me—forget that important aspect of teamwork.

When I first met Eugene Walker, I knew he was the right person to lead my construction company. He was my all-star, number one pick. A veteran of more than twenty-five years in the construction industry, Eugene has been a carpenter, field engineer, office engineer, project engineer, senior estimator, and project manager. He's helped build automobile plants, racetracks, office buildings, hospitals, hotels, college classrooms, rental car centers, and airport terminals. And he has been a champion and mentor for minorities in the construction industry.

If there is a Hall of Fame for the construction industry, I have no doubt that Eugene Walker is a shoo-in. (I've already volunteered to help him write his speech.) On top of all his credentials, awards, and honors, Eugene is a straight-up honest guy who will tell you exactly what he thinks even though it may not be what you want to hear. I respect that in a team member. In fact, I demand it in a team member.

I'm sure Eugene was wondering why I didn't listen to him when he warned me about hiring a certain subcontractor and I did it anyway. All I can say is that Eugene wasn't on my team at that point. He hadn't yet given notice to his previous employer, so my failure to heed his advice wasn't an official screwup by the boss. But it was still my bad. *Really* bad.

If you're in the process of building a team, I urge you to learn from my mistake. If you do your due diligence and hire smart, trustworthy people, listen to them. Take their advice. In this case, I was still trying to lure Eugene to my company, and I told him about a big job I'd landed. I wanted him to come on board and run that job, but he couldn't leave his previous employer on such short notice. So I told him that my other option was to hire a certain subcontractor to run the job.

Eugene advised me to wait for him before taking on such a big job with a subcontractor, but I made the decision to go ahead. And I soon learned that Eugene was right. I should have waited. I paid a price for that mistake when portions of the work had to be done over, so let me save you that expense in your business and in life as well.

If you want to live your dreams and achieve your purpose, don't try to go it alone. Instead, be intentional about building a strong team. Recruit people who will hitch to your wagon and take your business or your dreams to reality. If they don't buy into your dreams and goals, set them free to pursue their own. But when they do buy in, appreciate them. Show them that you value them, and tell them so too. And when they give you their thoughtful advice, do them the honor of listening. (You'll be doing yourself a favor.)

Never underestimate the value of investing in your relationships, whether it's in business, football, or life. Look beyond yourself to the greater good. And don't forget to say thank you.

Because no matter what your dream, no matter what your purpose, you won't get far without your team.

CHAPTER 8
ENHANCE YOUR ATTITUDE

*Now to him who is able to do immeasurably more
than all we ask or imagine, according to his power
that is at work within us, to him be glory.*

EPHESIANS 3:20-21

MY MANAGER AND MARKETING AGENT, Werner Scott, answered a cell phone call, and his face lit up as we drove into Atlanta the week before Super Bowl XXVIII in January 1994.

"What did you hear that made you so happy?" I asked.

"You're on the cover," he said.

"What cover?"

"*Sports Illustrated.* They put your picture on the front of their Super Bowl week issue."

"What?" I said. "You can't let that happen! Tell them they can't use my picture!"

Werner looked at me like I'd just canceled Christmas.

"Emmitt, this is an honor," he said. "You should be excited."

"I want nothing to do with the *Sports Illustrated* cover jinx, so get me off. I'm serious."

Every sports fan knows about the *Sports Illustrated* jinx. There is a long and scary list of athletes who've appeared on the cover only to die—or suffer injuries, losing streaks, or other bad breaks. Of course, many athletes who have appeared on that same cover have thrived, too. Michael Jordan made the cover forty-nine times. He did okay.

Even so, my initial reaction to Werner's news was not to press my luck. I didn't want anything messing up our shot at winning back-to-back NFL championships. (Obviously this was before I became a Christian and believed that God was in control of my destiny.)

Our Super Bowl opponents, the Buffalo Bills, were already fired up and looking for revenge because we'd embarrassed them 52–17 in the Super Bowl the year before.

I didn't want to fan those flames.

Or push my luck.

"You need to convince them to take my picture off the cover," I told Werner. "I don't need to be out there. Call them now. Tell them to put one of the Bills on the cover."

"No, they've already gone to press," said Werner. "So I suggest you change your attitude!"

Werner and I had been working together a long time. In fact, we are still working together because he is never afraid to give me a reality check—or an attitude adjustment—when I need one. And I definitely needed one in that moment.

There was nothing I could do at that point about the *Sports*

Illustrated cover. But, as Werner so bluntly pointed out, I could adjust my attitude about it. So I did.

Okay, it wasn't quite that easy.

I may have fussed and fretted a little more about the jinx, especially when I saw the headline they put on the cover shot—a game photo that showed me running past a defender's outstretched arm.

"The Unstoppable Emmitt Smith," it said.

Talk about fanning the flames and providing the other team with bulletin-board material! As if that weren't bad enough, the magazine's editors plastered their prediction of the upcoming Super Bowl's final score—"Dallas 24–Buffalo 17"—at the top of the cover page.

If there truly was a *Sports Illustrated* jinx, they were calling it out.

I'm really not a superstitious guy, though. More important, I am a firm believer in focusing on those things within my reach and leaving everything else to God. So after some initial stewing, I put the jinx out of my mind and focused on the game instead.

"You're right, Werner," I said. "I'm just going to go out there, do my best, and let God take care of the rest."

As it turned out, my attitude and my faith trumped the *SI* jinx.

We won the game 30–13. And thanks to my teammates, I had room to run for 132 yards and two touchdowns. I received both the Super Bowl MVP award and the NFL MVP award that year.

You and I may not ultimately control where we end up in life. God does that. But we do have the power to monitor our attitudes and adjust them as we go.

TAKING THE WHEEL

Let's take another minute to look back at where we've been.

- The dreams you have provide the vision.
- Your goals put you on the path to your purpose.
- Your strength of character and the principles and values you embrace keep you on course.
- Your courage and commitment move you beyond fear and past challenges.
- Embracing the right opportunities expands your reach.
- Supportive teammates can send you soaring.

Now, let's look at the ability to consciously choose your attitude in any given moment or situation.

God works from within you, through you, and for you when you choose to be enabled rather than disabled.

He works through you and for you when you choose to be grateful rather than hateful.

He works through you and for you when you choose to be humble and stay faithful.

The ability to consciously monitor and adjust your attitude is God's hand upon your hand, helping you find your way to his chosen path. People who take responsibility for and control of their attitudes are never stuck or locked in or powerless. When bad things happen, they always have at least one option: to choose a new attitude.

THE POWER TO CHOOSE

As it turned out, my photograph appeared on the cover of *Sports Illustrated* a total of thirteen times during my playing days. Thirteen! How lucky is that? If that jinx was meant to hit me, the folks at that magazine gave it plenty of opportunities. Even so, I managed to keep playing and thriving despite all those *SI* covers.

Fear of injury can cause just as much damage to a football player's career as a real broken arm or leg if it makes him overly cautious and keeps him from playing to the best of his abilities. The baseball player who takes a bad attitude into the batter's box can do more to hurt his chances than a pitcher could ever do. In the same way, a teacher who demeans her students or a lawyer who resents the power of a judge risks sabotaging a career because emotions are controlling his or her actions.

Letting your attitude and actions be guided entirely by your emotions is like taking your hands off the wheel of your car while speeding down the highway. You give up control. When I let my fear of the *Sports Illustrated* jinx get to me, Werner told me to put my hands back on the wheel and keep them there. He was reminding me that I had a choice to lose control or to take it.

My initial reaction seems silly in retrospect. In fact, Werner and I often laughingly refer to that incident when we catch each other being reactive instead of proactive. In fact, "I suggest you change your attitude!" has become a catchphrase for us, and a very useful one.

I encourage you to use it too. Remind yourself to change your attitude when

- fear drives self-destructive actions,
- anger boils inside you,
- failure seems like a finality,
- frustration overwhelms you,
- someone hurts you,
- a heavy workload intimidates you, or
- you can't get over a mistake.

All of those situations are very common experiences. Chances are, you have experienced quite a few—probably more than once. Some we might crash into a couple of times a day, right?

You are human, which means you are an emotional being. That's the way God made you. There is no shame in feeling fearful, angry, despairing, frustrated, hurt, intimidated, or guilty. As I noted earlier, emotions serve a purpose. If you don't feel them from time to time, you aren't living as richly as you should. Your emotions add to the depth of your experiences and relationships. They also give you information about yourself and how you are responding to the world around you. Emotions serve a purpose and should never be denied or ignored.

However, emotions don't need to be *obeyed*.

Once you've experienced and acknowledged an emotion, you can let it go and move forward by taking constructive action—to choose a positive mind-set instead of reacting emotionally. That's what it means to choose your attitude.

The truly unique thing about the power to choose our attitudes is that it is a universal power. It's not unique to any one of us or to a select group of us.

Most of the gifts God gives us are selectively distributed. For example, I was good at running from huge men in hard helmets. Then I discovered a gift for ballroom dancing. Now, I thrive at running a construction and commercial real-estate business. However, I can't draw a lick or sing a note on key. My small bundle of skills and talents helps make me who I am, just as yours helps to define you.

The diversity of God's people and the wide range of their gifts reflect his wisdom. Some of us run. Others block. Some play music. Others dance. Each of us has certain talents meant to help us fulfill a purpose for which God has made us uniquely qualified. We may lack other talents. Yet, we *all* have the ability to act rather than to react, the power to choose a response that puts us in control instead of allowing our emotions to control us.

There must be a very important reason that God gave all of us this ability. We know he always has a reason for what he does. In Ephesians 4:16 we're told, "He makes the whole body fit together perfectly. As each part does its own special work, it helps the other parts grow, so that the whole body is healthy and growing and full of love" (NLT).

I believe that's the answer. God gives us the power to choose our attitudes in order to keep us healthy and growing and full of God's love. Too often, though, we let our emotions dictate our attitudes and actions instead of using the power to take control. Our feelings catch us by surprise because we are distracted by the daily scramble at work and at home. The next thing we know, those feelings are in the driver's seat and we're headed for a crash. That's when we have to take back the wheel by adjusting our attitudes, tempering our emotions, and taking responsibility for our actions.

ATTITUDE ENHANCERS

I've already made the case that I am a very visual person. I have always prepared myself for challenges by "seeing" them in my mind and walking through my response. I do the same when it comes to adjusting my attitude. Nearly every time I find myself in a situation in which I need to change my attitude, my mind takes me back to my childhood home in Pensacola and our family room on weekend mornings when I was a little boy.

Like most kids, my brothers and sister and I watched cartoons on Saturday mornings. Often when a cartoon character was facing a choice between something good or bad, two tiny figures would appear, one on each shoulder. One was usually angelic, the other devilish. Both would whisper into the character's ears, trying to get him or her to do their bidding.

When I sense that my emotions are affecting my attitude, it helps me to visualize those cartoons and imagine the two sides battling it out on my shoulders. I can choose to listen to the devilish little guy on my shoulder, who is reactive and encourages me to act out of self-defeating emotions such as doubt and fear. Or I can tune in to the little angel, who is proactive and encourages me to act based on self-empowering mental habits such as humility, empathy, and gratitude.

Those last three, in fact, just happen to be my favorite attitude enhancers. I try to tune in to humility, empathy, and gratitude as often as I can for a very simple reason. They always seem to inspire a positive outcome even in challenging situations.

AN ATTITUDE OF HUMILITY

Earlier in this book I described Walter Payton as a "humble warrior" because despite his physical and mental toughness, he always seemed to put other people first. There was no big ego in Sweetness. He commanded attention and respect not by demanding it, but by earning it.

At some point, our society abandoned or lost touch with the connection between humility and leadership. Big egos and self-promoters seem to command all the attention of the media. In business, those who rise to power boast of the money they've made and the power they've wielded. Often they slash jobs while demanding huge bonuses even as their companies struggle or lose money. There is nothing humble about them.

What a contrast with Jesus, the Son of God, who lived in

poverty on this earth, ministering to the poor, the sick, and the sinful. We're told in the Bible that Jesus took on the "very nature of a servant" (Philippians 2:7). He even washed the feet of his disciples to show that serving others is what true leaders do.

You have to be strong to humble yourself like that. You have to have a powerful sense of purpose to lead by example and encouragement instead of command and control. You have to be really confident in who you are to voluntarily give up your right to command respect.

It takes strength to lead with humility—not insisting on your rights, putting yourself last. Just keep in mind that Jesus said in Mark 9:35 that "anyone who wants to be first must be the very last, and the servant of all."

Even modern-day experts on leadership like Jim Collins, the author of *Good to Great*, say that the best leaders in corporate America—those who lead their companies for many years and keep performing at high levels—are distinguished by their humility. The business leaders who rise to the top but quickly fall are those who become arrogant and put their own selfish needs first.

Is it possible to be a "servant leader" and still be a champion? I believe it is—although it isn't always easy. I see many good pastors and servant leaders who lead their congregations by example. Closer to home, my parents surely put their children first, working long hours and sacrificing their own goals and desires so that we might achieve ours. They taught us by their example, which is what great leaders and great parents do.

One of the experiences that Bishop Jakes and I shared as children still bonds us today. Like me, the bishop spent many hours tending to an ailing family member. In his case, it was his father. That is a life-changing experience for anyone, especially a child, because you learn about the fragility of life and the importance of putting others before yourself.

As a boy, I didn't give it much thought, but looking back I can see that I found it natural to take care of my ailing grandmother. After all, I grew up in a multigenerational family in which everyone looked out for one another. Some kids might have resented serving as a caretaker to an elderly family member. And as I've mentioned, I had moments when I struggled. After all, I was busy with football and school. I received a lot of attention because of my athletic ability. For the most part, though, I enjoyed spending those hours with my grandmother, helping her with meals and household chores. My nursing-home job also required that I sometimes assist elderly residents while cleaning toilets and keeping the grounds neat too.

Back then I never thought that it was a humbling experience. For me, it was about loving and caring for someone I loved and fulfilling my responsibilities in the family. (In the case of the nursing home, of course, it was also about making some spending money.) Looking back, though, I can see it was a very healthy thing for a young guy at that age to be asked to put someone else's needs ahead of his own.

Many young people become so focused on their own concerns about fitting in, being accepted, and figuring out who they are that they develop self-centered attitudes. I certainly wasn't immune to that. But when I got full of myself, someone always seemed to be there to adjust my attitude for me, if I didn't adjust it myself.

My high-school coach Dwight Thomas was always reliable in that respect. Despite our success on the field, he never let me become cocky. I've always kept in mind what he once told me: "The day you become satisfied and think that you know everything is the day you stop learning and the day you stop growing."

One of the great things about an attitude of humility is that this perspective allows you to laugh at yourself and at life's little twists and turns. Laughter is a great force for healing. When bad news seems to arrive at your doorstep by the busload, the ability to find humor in your situation can make a huge difference. Laughter can also be a balm for dented egos and wounded pride.

Shortly after I signed on to do *Dancing with the Stars*, I met my professional partner, Cheryl Burke, for the first time. She'd graciously agreed to come out to Virginia, where we were visiting Pat's family, for our first meeting and rehearsal. My attitude was already pretty humble because ballroom dancing was new turf for me. The only "ballroom" I'd ever been in was in a hotel where I was either receiving an award or giving one out. My dancing had been limited to making moves on the football field and the occasional dance with my wife.

I told Cheryl on that first meeting that she was the teacher and I was the student, but I was in this to win. I promised to do whatever it took to be the best partner she'd ever had. I wasn't bluffing, which is a good thing since Cheryl called me out right away. She handed me a pair of men's Latin dance shoes. She claims the heels were one and a half inches high. To me, they looked to be at least six inches.

"Do you think you can dance in these, Emmitt?" she asked.

"I think I can handle putting on a pair of shoes," I answered.

"Be careful," Cheryl warned. "You might have trouble walking in them at first."

I laughed as I laced the shoes up. My smile disappeared when I stood. I felt like I'd put on stilts. I don't know too many men who've had experience walking in heels like those, but I put on a brave face and busted a move.

Busted would be the operative word—as in "I busted my tail." I took one step and went down like a sack of potatoes. And did I mention that there was a camera crew present?

Sprawled on the floor, I had a range of options in choosing my attitude. Humiliation and embarrassment were early candidates. Anger was also available.

Finally I chose laughter—almost always a healthy choice.

After imagining what my pratfall must have looked like to Cheryl and the camera crew—especially following my cocky statement that I could handle the high-heeled shoes—I cracked up. The more I thought about it, the harder I laughed. Even after I managed to stand up and walk around a little, I could not stop laughing.

Once they saw that I wasn't hurt or ticked off, everyone else laughed too.

It could have been an ugly moment if I'd let my embarrassment, humiliation, or anger take hold of me. Instead, we all bonded in laughter, and I let Cheryl know that I didn't take myself too seriously.

I definitely had to grow accustomed to those high-heeled shoes before I had a walk—or any moves—worthy of the ballroom-dancing vocation I'd been called to on *Dancing with the Stars*. And that wouldn't be my last opportunity to laugh at myself. I believe that keeping an attitude of humility and good humor helped me stay in the competition and, eventually, win it with Cheryl.

We had a lot of fun working together on our routines, but it wasn't all fun and games, believe me. The stakes were high. The potential for embarrassing my partner, myself, and my family was always looming over me. Keeping "the unity of the Spirit through the bond of peace" (Ephesians 4:3) throughout all the training, rehearsing, and performing could be a challenge. But the more I managed to humble myself and laugh, the better it all went.

AN ATTITUDE OF EMPATHY

That same Bible passage I just mentioned, Ephesians 4, also refers to "bearing with one another in love" (verse 2), which is the apostle Paul's way of saying we should practice self-control, patience, love, and understanding with each other—especially when it isn't easy. What Paul is referring to is the very important and useful attitude of empathy.

You practice empathy by walking in the shoes of others, trying to understand their point of view before you judge them or even react to their words and actions. An attitude of empathy requires that you pay attention and understand not so much the words someone says to you, but the emotions behind the words. You have to listen with your heart and mind as well as with your ears.

This is the attitude the apostle James endorses in the Bible when he says that we must be "quick to listen, slow to speak and slow to become angry" (James 1:19). You don't have to be Mother

Teresa to have an attitude of empathy. This attitude really requires understanding and compassion, especially when someone close to you unleashes unkind or hurtful words.

In my experience, women are more naturally empathetic than men. Men are more likely to react to harsh words with anger or harmful actions, while women generally have the ability to move past anger to understanding more quickly. But women get tired and stressed out too. We're all capable of falling into an attitude of judgment at times.

Ephesians 4:31 tells us to "get rid of all bitterness, rage and anger, brawling and slander, along with every form of malice." Another way of putting that might be, "Don't get bitter. Get better." I'm sure you agree that this translates to wise advice in any language. I'm also sure you are thinking, *Easier said than done.*

If you took a popularity poll for attitudes, it's reasonable to assume that an attitude of anger and bitterness (which is the lingering taste of anger) would rank near the bottom. It's just not a very desirable way to be. Yet so many people carry that attitude around with them.

It's like smoking cigarettes. Virtually no one thinks smoking is good for you, yet even many successful and accomplished people continue to fill their lungs with toxic smoke and cancerous particles. An attitude of anger and bitterness is equally toxic. But all of us, at times, have given up control and allowed those dangerous emotions to guide our actions. The results are never pretty.

I've been known to lose my temper in the heat of battle on the football field and sometimes under the heat of the spotlight, too. I let loose, for example, when my former teammate Michael Irvin was twice passed up for the Hall of Fame. (Now my former teammate Charles Haley is going through the same thing.) My angry words were from the heart and intended to support my friend, a great athlete, so I don't regret them all that much. In fact, I thought he was being judged for things that were not football related. Still, he made it through in 2007, and I was grateful to join him a few years later.

I heard a wise man say that anger without action will leave us bitter and not better. I agree. But "action" doesn't mean we just let loose and lash out at others. A wiser choice would be to work out that angry energy through physical exercise or to write down your angry complaints and then throw the list away or even burn it. That way, you can move beyond it.

I'm a work in progress in this regard, as we all are. But I've looked for ways to control anger-driven attitudes, and I've had some success. One method for doing this is to counter anger and bitterness with an attitude of empathy and forgiveness.

It's not as difficult as it might sound. Instead of reacting emotionally, I take a step back, seek to rationally understand what happened, then respond thoughtfully and with control instead of flying off the handle. Once again, it is easier said than done, but it *can* be done by taking responsibility and control of your attitude.

Some may be tempted to think of empathy as a sign of weakness, but the truth is, an attitude of empathy can have a far more powerful effect than one of anger and bitterness. South Africa's heroic leader Nelson Mandela helped win better treatment for his fellow prisoners and eventually his own release from prison, in part by building empathy with the white Afrikaner guards and officials who held him captive for twenty-eight years. He did that by learning to speak their language and learning their culture and values so that he understood their motives and feelings. Mandela is a global hero because he defeated and overthrew a racist regime through the power of his empathy and the sheer force of his personality and character. South Africa—and the world—is better because of it.

I'm no Nelson Mandela, but I, too, have learned that empathy makes a big difference in my interactions with others. Cheryl Burke, who wrote about her struggles with self-esteem in her book, *Dancing Lessons*, credits me with helping her during our time together. One particular incident she cites occurred after we'd been working six or seven hours to master our paso doble routine.

The paso doble is a quick-stepping, dramatic dance style with moves reminiscent of bullfighting. And there was one particular twist-turn move in our routine that had me thinking a few choice words after a couple of hours of tripping over it. Then I started trying too hard, and that only made it worse.

After six hours of trying and failing to nail the move, I should have just called it a night and gone home to regroup. Instead, I kept pushing to get it right at least once before we went home. My mind wanted to take me where my body couldn't seem to go. I was frustrated by my inability to make the move, and so was Cheryl. We were sweating. We were tired and hungry. And our emotions were starting to get the best of us.

After messing up yet another time, I took a minute to wipe the sweat off my face, take a little walk around the rehearsal room, and compose myself. Cheryl, who was normally pretty patient, didn't say anything, but from her body language I could tell she was teed off with me. I was just as frustrated with myself.

I put myself in her shoes. How would I feel as a veteran running back if a rookie kept messing up a play in practice so that we couldn't go home after six hours on the field? Well, in this case, I was the rookie, and she was the veteran.

Cheryl went to the boom box and hit the play button to start the music.

"Let's go again," she said.

It was not a cordial invitation to dance.

We paso dobled just fine until it came time for my twist-turn, which I performed as more of a turn-twist.

"You've got to be kidding me!" Cheryl said. She then let loose with a curse word followed by "This is ridiculous." She stalked across the room to the boom box and shut off the music.

We stood there in silence. I took a minute to let my own anger and frustration pass.

I can't tell you exactly what all went through my mind in that moment. I didn't say anything, but there was a lot of conversation going on inside my head. I was angry with Cheryl for lashing out at me, but I certainly understood her frustration. This was an easy dance step for her.

I had to deal with my anger and frustration and, of course, my wounded male ego. Being knocked to the ground by a three-hundred-pound linebacker was easier to take than being cursed at by this tiny dancer. It's easy being a nice guy and a gentleman when people are friendly and respectful. This was a true test of my ability to adjust my attitude and take responsibility for my actions even as I warred with my feelings. Fortunately, my parents and grandparents raised me right, and my faith has made me strong.

Finally I walked over to Cheryl, looked her in the eye, and told her in a calm voice, "I understand that you're frustrated. But nobody talks to me like that. None of my football coaches ever spoke to me like that." (Well, maybe one or two of them did!) "Do we understand each other?" I asked.

She did. She apologized for taking her frustrations out on me. "Let's call it a night," I said.

The next morning, I nailed the twist-turn move. Then we did the routine again just to make sure I had it. We never again spoke of that moment when Cheryl lashed out, and our friendship and mutual respect grew stronger. She has said that she really respected me for responding to her angry words with calm empathy and understanding. She admits now that her own insecurities were the real trigger for her anger. She was frustrated that as the professional dancer she couldn't find a way to teach me how to do the twist-turn properly.

As it turned out, our resolution of that conflict led to Cheryl's being more patient and understanding with me as a student because I had shown patience and understanding with her. That's why an attitude of empathy can be a very powerful response. She benefited and I benefited, and the benefits paid dividends in the quality of our ongoing relationship and our performances as well.

Proverbs 12:16 says,

Fools show their annoyance at once,
  but the prudent overlook an insult.

I've had many moments in my life when I felt grateful for the caring people who raised me and for the God who guides me. That was certainly one of them. My emotions easily could have triggered an angry response to Cheryl's outburst, but I used what I'd been taught and the power of God within me to consciously take control of my response and to change my attitude from anger, bitterness, and hurt to one of empathy and understanding. Learning to do the twist-turn and mastering the paso doble were minor victories. Managing my emotions and adjusting my attitude in that moment provided me with a much bigger victory, a win-win for both student and teacher.

That was the only major meltdown Cheryl and I had, but there was one smaller area of disagreement having to do with my costume selections. Every week Cheryl would select her costume, and then I'd have to choose one that matched hers. The wardrobe team knew a little something about game on, so they kept bringing me tight-fitting, sleeveless shirts like those Mario Lopez had been wearing to highlight his muscular arms. But I kept saying no to those sleeveless shirts, which puzzled my partner too.

"C'mon, Emmitt. The fans are waiting for you to show off your muscles too," Cheryl said.

"Patience," I told her. "The other guys have all shown their stuff. They've tipped their hand, or at least their arms. If the fans are eager for me to show my guns, let's build up some anticipation and create a big moment."

I waited until the last week before the finals to bring out the big guns—wrapped in leopard-skin armbands. After that, poor Mario never had a chance!

AN ATTITUDE OF GRATITUDE

The impact of my induction speech at the Pro Football Hall of Fame surprised me. It seems to have resonated beyond the occasion and to still have an impact beyond my expectations. I often hear from men and women and schoolchildren who say my words that day touched and inspired them. There are also many references to the speech on inspirational and motivational websites.

Why did that speech touch people so much? I believe it's because the words obviously came from my heart and because I delivered it with a sincere attitude of gratitude.

I thank God for all his past blessings and all his future blessings too. I also take every opportunity to express my gratitude to those who've contributed to my success and happiness because I never know when I will see them again.

Life is a blessing. Even a bad day is one more day that you've had to fulfill your purpose and be a blessing to others. I encourage you to make a point of being thankful for each and every moment that you have, even those that seem more like burdens than blessings.

The Bible is packed with encouragement to express our gratitude and praise to God. For example, Psalm 95:2 says, "Let us come before his presence with thanksgiving, and make a joyful noise unto him with psalms" (KJV). Taking at least one moment each day to give thanks to God is a great way to center yourself before you go out and tackle the world. I also try to give thanks to God in prayer throughout the day, whenever I have a moment, wherever I am. That's the great thing about prayer. You don't even need a wireless connection. You can recharge spiritually without an electric outlet or power plug. You can't use your laptop or your cell phone on airplanes during takeoffs and landings, but you can pray—and believe me, I do.

When I express my gratitude and thanks in prayer, a sense of peace almost always comes over me. I feel cleansed and renewed in my relationship with Jesus, even more motivated to serve him and discover his purpose for me.

Giving thanks is important, but an attitude of gratitude is about more than expressing it in words and prayers. This attitude is really more about living in gratitude and finding a reason to be thankful in every moment, especially those moments that might otherwise give rise to negative attitudes driven by anger, fear, frustration, despair, and hurt.

We all have the power to disarm those potentially negative emotions by choosing to be thankful. Some life coaches and psychologists call this "reframing" because it involves taking an event that seems to be dark or negative and choosing to look at it differently, as if it were a picture in a completely different frame. Doing this is much easier than it sounds, and you might be surprised at how effective it can be.

I was reminded of this one day while I was talking to a friend about our crazy household. Pat and I have a large blended family. We each have daughters from previous relationships, and we have three children together. They range in age from teenagers to toddlers. As you might guess, ours is a very lively household. I described our daily chaos to my friend, who is older than me, and he reframed the situation for me.

"I used to complain about my kids' toys being everywhere, their rooms being a mess, and their music blaring all over the house," he said. "But now that they've all grown up and moved out, I miss the chaos and the noise. So my advice to you is to embrace it and to be grateful for your kids' presence in your house while they are there. They will be gone sooner than you think."

Now mind you, I hadn't been complaining about our children, merely noting that our household isn't a place of much peace and quiet. Even so, this friend shifted my perspective and adjusted my attitude to one of gratitude. Ever since then, when I walk into a roomful of kids who are carrying on as kids tend to do, I am not the least bit inclined to tell them to quiet down or send them outside to play. Instead, I say a little prayer of thanks to God for blessing us with their presence in our lives.

An attitude of gratitude really is an all-purpose cleanser. You can wipe away just about any frustration, fear, or fret with a simple application. (I should do infomercials for this attitude.) There are so many ways you can put this attitude to work to improve the quality of your life.

Let's say you are driving to an important meeting and suddenly traffic comes to a stop. You turn on the radio and learn there has been an accident a few miles up the road. There is no exit, so you have to wait it out—creeping along, starting and stopping.

The emotions that normally arise in this sort of situation are not positive, are they? You worry about being late for your meeting or missing it altogether, which brings stress. Then come fears about the repercussions of missing the meeting—more stress.

Anger is another likely suspect for this scenario. *Why did this have to happen now? Why here?* Even more stress.

Those are all typical and natural responses to being stuck in traffic while traveling to an important meeting. Yet none of them will do you any good. Worrying, being fearful and angry, and stressing out will simply wear on your body and mind without changing the circumstances one bit. Nothing good comes of those emotions and the negative attitudes they can instill. In fact, it's likely that if you keep sitting in your car with an attitude of resentment or an attitude of frustration, you might do something to make matters worse. You might slam your hand on the steering wheel and break a finger. Or you might shout a curse word out the window and offend the motorcycle cop alongside your car.

But what if you made a "joyful noise" instead?

You are probably thinking that there is not much to be grateful for when you are late for an important meeting because the highway is shut down. But as my friend Werner would say, "You need to change your attitude." And when you do, you'll be able to find all sorts of things to be grateful for while you are stuck in traffic. Here are a few suggestions from your friendly attitude-adjustment agent.

First, there are scenario-specific reasons to be thankful. For instance, I can be grateful that

- I was not involved in the accident that is tying up traffic,
- my car has plenty of fuel,
- my car's air conditioner or heater is working,

- the cars behind me slowed down and stopped instead of crashing into me,
- the police and rescue vehicles are on the scene,
- it's not raining/snowing/icy,
- I have my cell phone and I can call those I'm meeting to tell them I'll be delayed because of a traffic tie-up,
- this will give me more time to prepare for the meeting, and
- this meeting represents a good opportunity.

Then there are more general reasons for gratitude in this situation and similar scenarios that might provoke the same negative emotions. For instance, even though I'm stuck in traffic and late for my meeting, I can be grateful

- for my health and the good health of my loved ones,
- for the opportunity to provide a comfortable life for my family,
- that my life is blessed with supportive friends,
- that I have strong faith that helps me deal with challenges and circumstances beyond my control, and
- for this day and every day I'm allowed to pursue God's plan for me.

I'm sure you can come up with your own reasons to adjust to an attitude of gratitude now that you understand the frame of mind and the process. There is remarkable power in this particular attitude adjustment. I can tell you from experience that an attitude of gratitude can even help win football games in the NFL.

The Dallas Cowboys faced a significant challenge in our first game of the 1992 regular season. We had to play the defending Super Bowl champions, the Washington Redskins. Now, aside from the historical conflict between cowboys and Indians, our rivalry with the Redskins runs deep.

Few people today realize that the man who first put an NFL team in Dallas in 1960 or so, Texas oilman Clint Murchison, had been aced out in an earlier attempt to buy the Redskins from then-owner George Preston Marshall. When Marshall tried to change the terms of the deal at the last minute, Murchison canceled the deal and then decided to start his own team in Dallas. The NFL expansion committee, led by George Halas, the famed "Papa Bear" from Chicago, supported Murchison's bid. So did all of the other NFL owners except Redskins owner Marshall, who apparently did not practice any kind of a positive attitude toward Murchison.

But the Texas oilman had a trick up his sleeve. He'd managed to buy the rights to the music for the Redskins' beloved fight song, whose lyrics had actually been written by Marshall's wife. Marshall had to agree to approve the NFL franchise in Dallas before Murchison would give the rights back to him. So I guess you could say that the Cowboys came to Dallas for a song.

The rivalry between the two teams has been strong ever since. *Sports Illustrated* once named it the strongest in the NFL. The Cowboys and Redskins are two of the most successful and wealthiest franchises in the league, and they play each other twice a year. In September of 1992 when we faced the Redskins in our season opener, they were spoiling for a fight. Although they had won the Super Bowl that January, we had ruined their shot at a perfect record for the 1991 season by handing them their first loss after they'd gone undefeated for the first eleven weeks.

The Cowboys had ended the 1991 season 11–5, so we came into the new season feeling confident. The Redskins, with their Super Bowl trophy in hand, were every bit as confident, and they wanted to take revenge on us for ruining their shot at a perfect season. I was feeling good because I'd won the NFL rushing title for the previous season. But I didn't want to rest on my laurels. I wanted to build upon that achievement, and I really wanted our team to beat Washington in the opener. So I put my attitude of gratitude to work.

Just before game time on September 7, I sneaked around our locker room and dropped Rolex watches into the lockers of each of our offensive linemen—the guys who clear the path for me to run. Each of the watches was inscribed with this message: "Thanks for the 1,563 rushing yards: NFL Rushing Title. Emmitt Smith."

Now, you might say it was just coincidence or that my expression of gratitude was not a major factor. But that day we beat the Washington Redskins, the reigning Super Bowl champs and our historic rival, by a score of 23–10. Our offensive linemen opened up such big holes in their defense that I ran for 140 yards. We went on to end the 1992 season 13–3 and to win the Super Bowl. And our linemen played so well that season that I won the NFL rushing title for that year too.

That's the power of an attitude of gratitude!

Just imagine what it can do for you if you remember to sing:

Make a joyful noise unto the LORD, all ye lands.

Serve the LORD with gladness: come before his presence
    with singing.

Know ye that the LORD he is God: it is he that hath made us,
    and not we ourselves; we are his people, and the sheep of
    his pasture.

Enter into his gates with thanksgiving, and into his courts with
    praise: be thankful unto him, and bless his name.

For the LORD is good; his mercy is everlasting; and his truth
    endureth to all generations.

PSALM 100:1-5 (KJV)

CHAPTER 9
DECIDE WISELY

Trust in the L<small>ORD</small> with all your heart;
do not depend on your own understanding.
Seek his will in all you do,
and he will show you which path to take.

PROVERBS 3:5-6, NLT

I HAD NOTHING TO LOSE and everything to gain. But I was still as nervous as a rookie on the first day of training camp when my cards were dealt at the start of the National Heads-Up Poker Championship in Las Vegas. I had a sponsor, so I didn't put my own money in the pot, but I was playing for pride—and a $750,000 grand prize.

The other players in the 2011 tournament at Caesars Palace were pros who play poker every day and every night. I'm sure they play in their sleep, too. They bluff for a living.

In other words, I was way out of my league. I've played some before, but I'm definitely not a pro. And my nerves were on edge because I have one major challenge in playing cards: my face.

I do not have a poker face. I have a face that might as well be a Kindle or an iPad because most of the time people can read me like a book. Happy, sad, and everything in between, my face wants to light up with whatever I'm feeling. You know the saying about people wearing their emotions on their sleeve? Mine are displayed just below my forehead. My mug is my personal JumboTron for displaying my moods.

This was not a liability when I was wearing a football helmet or dancing with the stars, but my facial expressiveness can pose a problem in any card game that requires bluffing, whether it's old maid or Texas hold 'em.

Professional poker players are really expert decision makers. They know the odds and constantly recalculate them in their minds before deciding how to play their hands. But that's not their only tool for deciding what to do. They also read their opponents for "tells."

In other words, the pros at the poker table aren't just good with cards. The top players say they often can tell what sort of hand an opponent is holding just by looking at the person, not the cards. They can read facial expressions, gestures, body language, nervous habits, and other unconscious signs that give away what their opponents are thinking. Certain top players have been known to study the big veins on the side of their opponents' heads to monitor their blood-pressure changes.

That ability to read people gives the poker pros an edge in deciding when to hold 'em and when to fold 'em. There is still an element of luck involved, but professional poker players bring so much skill to the table that raw luck is much less a factor for them than the typical amateur.

Especially one with a Kindle face.

When I play against the pros, I have to psych myself into a "nerves of steel" mode, and I mentally put on a mask to make my feelings less obvious. In the opening round of this tournament, I was paired against David Williams, one of the most successful poker players of all time and a member of an all-star crew called Team PokerStars Pro. He finished second in the World Series of Poker a few years ago, winning $3.5 million, and in 2010 he'd won a $1.53 million pot as the World Poker Tour champion.

I must have done an okay job of blanking out my expressions because I hung in there against David for a long stretch in that first round. I had some luck catching really good cards on the final draw a couple of times, which is called "finding a miracle on the river." Thanks to my mask, a few miracles, and a little skill, I somehow managed to beat the reigning World Poker Tour champ to score a huge upset that sent me into the next round.

The poker bloggers called it "the shocker of the day." Nobody was more shocked than me! But I wasn't about to get cocky—especially since my next opponent was poker pro Andrew Robl. That man was a card-playing machine. He reminded me of a robot in the way he kept staring at me, almost as if he had laser vision. He must have figured out the Kindle face thing because he looked at my mug more than he ever looked at his cards. I'm sure I was giving away some things because he was making me really nervous. It felt like he was reading my soul! I almost burst out laughing a couple of times because his glare made me so nervous.

I hung in there for a while with Andrew Robl, but then he drew a straight, and my day was done. I was knocked out of the tournament, and he went on to finish third, taking home $125,000.

One thing I learned about poker is that it's all about making smart decisions.

The lives we lead are the product of the decisions we make. To live at the championship level you need to understand that the decision-making process is critical to your success.

But before we go on to explore decision making, let's review once more:

- Your vision for your life is inspired by your dreams.
- The path to your purpose is determined by the goals you create to follow your dreams.
- You stay on course by using your principles and values as road markers that define your character.
- You move beyond fear and challenges with courage and commitment.
- You keep growing and expanding your reach by recognizing or creating opportunities.
- You build a team of supporters and encouragers who help you achieve more than you might have ever done alone.
- You consciously choose positive attitudes that allow you to be proactive rather than reactive.

And all along the way, of course, you have to make some decisions.

Your decisions really do determine the course your life takes as you follow God's plan. Each major decision is another step in that journey, so you must have a thoughtful process for measuring the distance before you take a leap and make sure you have a safe place to land.

Every successful person I know has a carefully designed process for making decisions, one that suits his or her personality. Yours may differ from mine, and that's fine. In this chapter I'll provide you with a basic framework that you can refine and adjust to suit your personal needs and desires.

The critical thing is for you to intentionally create a process for making decisions so that you don't approach potentially life-changing moments in a haphazard manner—because there are no guarantees you'll get a do over. Yes, people sometimes do get second chances in life. And God in his grace can bring something good out of even the most disastrous decisions. But decisions can still have powerful and often unavoidable consequences. So it only makes sense to approach decisions, especially high-stakes decisions, as though you only have one shot.

Mastering the facts, weighing the pros and cons of each option, getting a perspective from two or three angles to reduce the risks, learning from your mistakes, and then making the leap, all contribute to a good decision-making process, whether the decision involves playing cards, building relationships, or running a business.

Yes, people sometimes do get second chances in life. And God in his grace can bring something good out of even the most disastrous decisions. But decisions can still have powerful and often unavoidable consequences. So it only makes sense to approach decisions, especially high-stakes decisions, as though you only have one shot.

There is also a spiritual component involved in each step of my decision-making process. I recommend that you ask for God's guidance in your decision process too. I find the Bible verse my grandmother gave me to take to college especially useful when making big decisions and little ones as well:

Trust in the LORD with all your heart;
do not depend on your own understanding.
Seek his will in all you do,
and he will show you which path to take.

PROVERBS 3:5-6, NLT

You and I don't know what God has in store for us. Yet I feel confident in saying that his plans exceed even our grandest dreams. As someone who grew up in the lowly Pensacola projects and now finds himself building big-city high-rises, I feel *extremely* confident in telling you that you must never, ever expect anything but great things for your life. Jeremiah 29:11 backs me up on this: "'For I know the plans I have for you,' declares the LORD, 'plans to prosper you and not to harm you, plans to give you hope and a future.'"

God definitely has a plan for you, but that doesn't mean you can coast through life, letting him do all the work. He will teach you and test you. And those tests and lessons will often come when you are standing at a crossroads, trying to decide which road to take. You can't stand there forever and wait for God to send you a sign. (In rare instances, he *might* do that, but he's a lot more likely to guide you through the process of making your own decision.)

So you'll need a process for making your decisions thoughtfully. Here are some of the steps that have been helpful to me.

TAKING MEASURE

The first step in basic decision making is to look at the facts so that you totally understand what your options are, what the situation is, and how much time you have to make the decision. If another person or business is involved—for example, if you are negotiating a contract of some sort—you'll also need to consider what the other party's motives, needs, and goals are.

I was still college age when I entered into my first major contract negotiation as a first-round draft pick of the Dallas Cowboys. The guy on the other side of the table was a multimillionaire businessman renowned for his hard-nosed, penny-pinching negotiating style. Jerry Jones had played football for the Arkansas Razorbacks and then built his fortune in the rough-and-tumble, high-risk oil and gas exploration business. He didn't make millions by throwing money around. He'd once said, "I'd walk across Texas for five dollars," and nobody thought he was bluffing.

When he said that, he was talking about negotiating with me.

My rookie contract was cut in a high-stakes poker game, to be sure. And it was the first major financial decision of my life. I hired an experienced sports agent, Richard Howell, to represent me in negotiations, but even then, I did not give up control or responsibility. I felt this was simply too important a decision to hand it over to someone else.

But I also felt it was important to admit what I didn't know and then to hire someone whose expertise and experience made up for what I lacked. As Proverbs 15:22 says,

> *Plans fail for lack of counsel,*
>   *but with many advisers they succeed.*

It's always smart to seek wise counsel when a big decision looms. This might include Internet research, trips to the library, and also talking to a variety of people who might be able to offer you information and wisdom. If possible, seek out experts in the fields that pertain to your decision. If you can't afford professional help, look to your local colleges and universities for experts in the academic ranks or within professional organizations and service groups like the local chamber of commerce, Young Presidents' Organization, and SCORE (a consulting resource for small businesses).

It may also help to talk to people who have walked the path you hope to take. If, for example, you have a decision to make on a job offer, talk to people who work or have worked for the potential employer. Find out how they liked working there and what the benefits and salary ranges are. If possible, try to learn what lies on the other side of your decision.

Don't forget to consult your trusted friends and advisers, those who care about you and have your best interests at heart—as well as anyone, like your spouse, whose welfare may be affected by your decision. It may even be a good idea to talk to a counselor who can help you step back and look at the long-range implications of each option.

I have always sought counsel from my family and close friends in addition to working with sports agents and marketing consultants. And I try to listen well to what they say. However, I would never let any of these counselors make the final decision for me. At some point, I have to step up and take responsibility for my decisions. After all, I'm the one who will have to live with the consequences. Of course, if you are in a relationship and the decision will affect both of you, both parties need to be in agreement.

Accepting responsibility for your decisions will motivate you to gather as much information as possible so that you can decide wisely. You need to be able to support your decision with facts.

In the case of my rookie contract, I also needed to fully understand the position of Jerry Jones and the Cowboys.

From their point of view, they'd chosen me as the seventeenth pick in the 1990 draft. Sixteen other teams had passed on me. There were still doubts as to whether I was big enough or fast enough to play in the NFL. They felt there was considerable risk involved.

The Cowboys made an initial offer to me of $3.2 million for five years. I did not want to be tied up in a contract for that long. After studying the salaries of other running backs and rookies around the league, I had decided to seek $3.2 million for two years, figuring that in those two years I would prove myself and then come back to the table for a much higher amount.

The Cowboys' tactic, called "slotting," was to say they were paying me what was typical for a seventeenth pick in the NFL draft. Unfortunately for them, Jerry Jones had said in a radio interview that the Cowboys originally had ranked me fourth in the draft, so if that was the game they were playing, I felt they had to pay me a salary appropriate for that higher slot.

In measuring my situation, I wasn't without some serious ammunition. In three seasons at Florida, I'd set fifty-eight school records. I'd been an all-American in high school. I knew what was in my heart, and I was certain I would bring a whole new dimension to the Cowboys' offense. So I didn't take the first offer Jerry Jones put out there.

Jerry responded the way you'd expect a tough negotiator to respond. He bluffed and blustered, playing the media by casting me as difficult and demanding, and blasting my agent as "a hold-out agent." Since Jerry was making noise but not offers, I opted not to attend training camp. No pay, no play. Jerry and his team didn't seem to be in any hurry to come back to the table, so I went home to Pensacola.

The negotiations went back and forth for the entire summer. When I still didn't have a contract by late August, my parents began to worry that I'd made the wrong decision to leave college before my senior year.

I was determined not to panic and make a decision I'd regret for the next five years. Patience isn't always possible when faced with a major decision, but I'd never advise rushing the process if you can help it. There was intense pressure on me to sign this rookie contract—from the outside and from within. The Cowboys' coaches, players, and fans wanted me on board so I could prepare for the coming season. I wanted to be well schooled on the Dallas offense and on top of my game physically and mentally for my first NFL season. And, of course, I was looking at the sort of money that would dramatically change my life and the lives of my parents too.

We cut a deal for a three-year contract that paid $3 million, including nearly a million upon signing. I'd held out for forty-eight days—the longest rookie holdout in Cowboys history at the time. This is nothing to be proud of, but it had to happen.

A reporter once wrote, "The iron will Emmitt Smith showed during his holdout served him well in his NFL career." He got that right.

Every critical decision you make has an impact on the rest of your life. In this case, my rookie holdout didn't just bring me contract terms that were much closer to what I wanted. It also sent the message for future negotiations that I knew my value and was willing to fight for what was right. I had to be strong in my first series of contract negotiations with the Cowboys because those negotiations set the tone for all future dealings with them and with any other NFL teams I might play for. They were also valuable preparation for my future life as a businessman.

WEIGHING YOUR OPTIONS

When you are preparing to make a major decision, a big part of your responsibility is to look at all the options available to you and to measure each option against your long-term goals. As much as I loved competing, I had always seen football as the means to an end. My goal was to earn a college degree that would prepare me for life after football. So returning to campus wasn't just a bluff. It was a viable option for me. It was also an option that my parents approved of because they put a high value on education.

When it came to my contract negotiation, I had to keep in mind that having such viable options gave me leverage. The

Cowboys were well aware that I could just decide to reject their offer, go back to school to earn my degree, then market my talents to other teams or to the business world. (Although let's be real—there wasn't a degree in the world that would have paid me $3.2 million!)

When you weigh your options before making a big decision, you might find it helpful to write them all down and then list the pros and cons of each option. Choose only those options that are in alignment with your principles and values and set you up to achieve your long-term goals.

Again, don't be afraid to talk through each option with people you trust. If you can find someone older who has successfully walked the path you hope to take, ask that person for advice. Though the final choice is yours to make, you don't have to make a decision in a vacuum.

Once you've examined your options thoughtfully, make a list of those that make the most sense. Then choose the one that stirs your heart and soul. One of the keys to lifelong happiness and success is to do what you love while making a living from it. So don't ever make a decision purely for money or out of a sense of duty if you can help it. Go with your heart, but only after doing everything within your power to reduce your risk.

REDUCING RISK

Every decision you make involves some level of risk. Rarely can you eliminate it, but you can often reduce it quite a bit through diligent research and by looking at the decision from a variety of perspectives. I try to examine the risk level of my business and personal decisions from three different perspectives—the first person, the second person, and the third person.

I first consider the risks from my personal point of view. Then I'll look at them from the point of view of any other parties involved. And finally I'll go to the "third person" by stepping back and assessing the risk as a disinterested third party.

Granted, sometimes it's impossible to be that detached. In those cases, I'll look for advisers who don't have a stake in the game and ask for their assessment.

In my commercial real-estate deals, risk mitigation begins with doing due diligence to determine the true value and condition of an asset I am considering for development. Whether it is a ten-story building or a vacant lot, I look at the neighborhood, the traffic patterns, the infrastructure, the terms of the lease or purchase, whether I will self-finance or borrow money, what improvements can be made at what cost, the available parking, and many other factors. You might say I'm always looking for the snake in the woods by asking what factors in the deal have the potential to jump out and bite me.

Most of the time, I find, it's all in the details. Hone in on the small print and every facet and factor when assessing the risk in your big decisions, in both business and relationships. Remember, there is risk on both sides of a decision. There is the risk of making a choice and the risk of not doing anything. Sometimes, the wisest decision might be to walk away. If your heart isn't in it, walk away. If the risk is too great, walk away. If your principles and values and goals aren't in alignment, walk away.

When making major decisions or conducting critical negotiations, it really helps to approach them from an abundance perspective rather than a scarcity perspective. If you believe in abundance, you believe that there are unlimited opportunities awaiting you. An abundance mentality will help you make thoughtful and patient decisions because you always believe that other opportunities will present themselves. You'll do your best to reduce risk, of course, but the stakes won't seem quite as high, and you'll be able to take fear out of the equation.

Never, ever make a decision based on fear, whether it's fear that you'll never get another opportunity, fear of failure, or fear of looking silly. Fear must not be part of the decision-making process. If you feel that your fears are affecting your decision making, call a time-out, and then do whatever it takes to manage that fear.

I kept this in mind at the end of my third season with the Cowboys, when it came time to negotiate a new contract. Before the start of the 1993 season, Jerry Jones and his team made me an initial offer of $9 million for a four-year contract. I countered with a demand for $15 million. Game on.

I'd sent a message with my long rookie holdout that I was a determined negotiator, so Jerry came out with his guns blazing this time. He made some noise about trading me if I didn't take his initial offer.

He was bluffing. Or at least I thought he was.

After my first season with the Cowboys, I'd been named NFL Offensive Rookie of the Year. In my second season, I had led the entire league in rushing. In my third, I'd again led the league in rushing and we'd won the Super Bowl. I'd been the first Cowboy running back named as the Super Bowl MVP, and at the time no other running back had ever been rushing leader for the season and won the Super Bowl too.

On top of all those accomplishments and honors, I'd never missed a game in my first three seasons. So in assessing their side of the deal, I had to think that the Cowboys were risking a lot by threatening to trade me.

But Jerry Jones had a wild card. He knew I wasn't a free agent who could sell his services to the highest bidder in the open market. Because of a new collective bargaining agreement just put in place by the league, I was a "restricted" free agent.

Bad for me. Good for Jerry.

The new agreement and my restricted status meant I could negotiate with twenty-nine other teams in the league for just one month. Then the window would close and I could only negotiate with the team that owned my rights, the Dallas Cowboys. In addition, the Cowboys had the right to match any offer I received from any other team.

After performing at such a high level in my first three seasons, you might think that I'd find a long line of NFL teams at my door offering me contracts. Funny how that worked. Not one contacted me, even after I'd identified those warm-weather teams that I was willing to play for.

I finally called Coach Don Shula of the Miami Dolphins and asked him to make me an offer. "You need a running back to go with Dan Marino, and I could help you get to the next Super Bowl," I said.

Shula didn't disagree. Instead, he gave me a reality check and a risk update. "Any offer I make you will just be matched by Jerry Jones anyway. And if I make you a huge offer, my own players will wonder why they didn't get it."

Now I saw what I was up against. All the other teams felt that Jerry Jones would match any offer they made, so why throw out a big-money offer and set the bar higher for future negotiations with their own players? Thanks to that mentality, I had much less leverage in my negotiations for a new Cowboys contract. They were the only team across the table.

Again, I weighed the risks and finally offered a prayer: "God, I did all I needed to do, so now I need you to work this out."

I told my sports agent and his team to keep me in the loop. Then I headed home to Pensacola to work out, chill out, and enjoy some time with my family. I hoped the news photos showing me working out on the beach, playing video games at my parents' house, and hanging out in my Pensacola sports memorabilia store would send a message to the Cowboys' owner. I also let it be known that going back to Gainesville to pick up some more college credits was an option too.

Jerry knew I was serious about earning a diploma and preparing for a life after football. He had admitted that he respected my determination and the fact that I'd been very involved in my rookie negotiations instead of just turning everything over to my agent. That, too, factored into my risk assessment for this big decision and major negotiation.

I knew Jerry respected me as a person and a player. But that didn't mean he wouldn't go after the best deal possible, even if it meant trading me. The Cowboys' owner was well aware that his quarterback, Troy Aikman, would be negotiating a new contract soon and that Aikman's agent would base his salary demands in part on the outcome of my deal. That situation, too, needed to figure into my risk assessment.

All things considered, though, my risk was much lower than it had been during my rookie contract negotiations. Then I'd been an unknown commodity as far as the NFL was concerned. I'd been one of the top running backs in the draft, of course. Sportswriters had cast me as the hardworking kid from a low-income family, David to Jerry's Goliath, and the fans had supported me in that role. Their support had given me a little more leverage in negotiations—not much, but a little. But there'd still been considerable risk in holding out too long as a rookie because I'd never played in an NFL game. The Cowboys had felt they were taking a bit of a gamble on me despite my record-breaking college performance. After all, many top college players have difficulty adjusting to the more intense competition in the NFL.

Now, after three years in the league, I had clout, which helped reduce the risk of holding out for a better deal. Jerry knew I'd been busy developing other revenue streams, including major endorsement deals with big brands like Coca-Cola, Reebok, and Starter. My rushing titles, my Pro Bowls, and the value of my own brand as an athlete and individual of good character also were undeniable factors.

Then there was the emotional element. I was a fan favorite and a solid citizen, and I'd already helped put a Super Bowl ring on Jerry's finger. He loved that ring, and for all of his posturing and posing, he knew I wasn't a luxury. Most of the experts felt that if the Cowboys wanted to keep on winning Super Bowls, they needed me on the field.

That became especially clear when the season started and my contract still hadn't been resolved. They had to start without me—and the first game was against our archrivals, the Washington Redskins, in DC. My replacement was a rookie, Derrick Lassic, a fourth-round pick out of the University of Alabama. Being thrown into such a big role so early in his career was a difficult challenge for Derrick, and everyone knew he was receiving a baptism under fire.

The Cowboys lost to the Redskins 35–16. I felt bad for my teammates, and I knew losing to Washington had hit Jerry where it hurt the most. But still, he didn't call me with a better offer.

Next the Cowboys faced our former Super Bowl rivals, the Buffalo Bills, and suffered another tough loss, 13–10.

My teammates made no bones about missing me, and they let Jerry Jones know how they felt. After the loss to Buffalo, our star defensive end, Charles Haley, who had two Super Bowl rings from his days with the San Francisco 49ers, smashed his helmet through a locker room wall with Jerry standing right there. Jerry got his point.

The owner's leverage on me was slipping, and his risk level was climbing. So was the pressure for him to sign me. The sportswriters were unloading on him. They didn't mince words. "Without Emmitt Smith the Cowboys are Tampa Bay," wrote *Washington Post* columnist Mike Wilbon. "They stink."

I didn't agree with that assessment of my team, but there was no doubt that the pressure was now on Jerry to bring me back. I'd been working out, running and lifting weights in Pensacola. I was in great shape and eager to return to competition, but my negotiating team made it clear that I was willing to sit out the entire season. Then I would be able to put my services up for bid as an unrestricted free agent, which would surely bring some lucrative offers from other teams. My value in a free market, according to some estimates, could be as much as $25 million.

Jerry had to make a move, and he did. He offered $13.4 million for four years. But I wanted to keep pushing because now the momentum was mine. I turned down that offer and told Jerry I was preparing to return to Dallas, but only to pick up my Super Bowl ring, which had arrived from the manufacturer. I told him I intended to clear out my locker and return to Pensacola.

After suffering two losses and taking a beating in the media, Jerry had little choice but to sweeten the pot. He offered me a $4 million signing bonus and another $3 million in other bonuses, as well as adding another $200,000 to the overall contract. The total made me the highest-paid running back in the NFL.

I still feel that offer was too low. It should have been around $20 million. But given all the circumstances, I felt this was an acceptable offer that would set me up for an even bigger payday down the road. And, as you no doubt have figured out, I was ready to return to the football field.

ALWAYS LEARNING

One thing that being an athlete teaches you is that losing is part of winning. If I had let every loss send me into despair and depression, mine would have been a very short career. This principle applies to life as well and is worth remembering, because while some of your decisions will work out beautifully, others may not. You must learn to savor your victories and your losses alike because both provide the opportunity to grow through experience.

That's a major key in making good decisions, in fact. Do your best to learn from every step of the decision-making process, even from your mistakes. That way you'll always be improving your game, whatever that game might be. In poker and in life, you can't really control what cards you are dealt, so you have to do everything possible to master the strategies and the nuances of the game. Your mistakes can bring you closer to that mastery if you determine to learn from them.

I've made mostly good decisions in my life, and I'm always glad I made them myself, even those that have not turned out well. Why? Because even with my bad decisions, I've learned something positive, something that has helped me make better decisions and be a better football player, a better businessman, or a better man.

TAKING THE LEAP

Once you've done all you can to put the odds in your favor, then you will need to decide whether to make a leap or stay put. In either case, I advise you to try to make a final review session part of every major decision you make.

Whenever possible, I like to sit down and list all that I had hoped to accomplish when I first set out to make a decision. Then I note whether I accomplished those goals, exceeded them, or fell short. And finally, I write down what I learned and what I might do better in making my next big decision.

Looking back, the decisions I made in negotiating that second contract with the Dallas Cowboys worked out well, given the challenges I faced as a restricted free agent. In the end, the risk of a losing season, the risk of losing me to the free-agent market, and the pressure from fans and sportswriters all were factors in Jerry's decision to offer me a better deal. He has acknowledged that over the years in many interviews. The Cowboys' season and the team's future were in jeopardy after we lost the first two games, so his risk in not signing me was increased considerably.

In the meantime, I had managed to reduce my own risk by establishing myself as the league's premiere running back, by never missing a game in my first three seasons, by being a good team member and community representative, and by having attractive options in the free market if the Cowboys did not sign me. By the time Jerry's $13.6 million offer for four years hit the table, I had very little risk involved in my decision. I was still a healthy young man with the potential for ten more years of high earnings and high performance as a football player.

Jerry made a wise decision, and when that 1993 season ended, he had another Super Bowl ring to prove it.

And so did I.

CHAPTER 10

BE THE BLESSING YOU SEEK

For unto whomsoever much is given,
of him shall be much required.

LUKE 12:48, KJV

PAT AND I FIRST MET Prentice Richmond in 2010 at a friend's reception for the Children's Defense Fund of Texas. The CDF is one of the nonprofit organizations we support through our Pat & Emmitt Smith Charities. Prentice, a high-school senior from Dallas, had been selected for one of the local CDF's three $20,000 Beat the Odds scholarships. The college scholarship winners are selected because they've overcome considerable challenges to become top students and high achievers.

Prentice didn't offer much about his family background at our first meeting, but we did learn that he was captain of his high-school football team, worked as a coordinator for the city police department's youth athletic league, and volunteered at CitySquare (formerly Central Dallas Ministries). He was a very polite and thoughtful young man who charmed everyone he spoke to that night. Pat was particularly impressed with him, saying his smile reminded her of me. (Pat is such a wise woman!)

The day after we met Prentice, we drove to attend a CDF luncheon. The minute we walked in the door, one of the organizers approached us in tears.

"You won't believe what we found out about Prentice last night," she said. "He had nowhere to go after the reception. Turns out, he's homeless."

We knew that Prentice came from a troubled inner-city home, but we'd had no idea that this young man's challenges included feeding, clothing, and sheltering himself. In fact, he'd been on his own for several years.

Pat and I were stunned—and touched—to learn about Prentice's plight. In fact, Pat cried too as she thought of the young man's charm and upbeat personality during our meeting. "He didn't know where he would be sleeping that night, but he didn't let that wear on him at all," she said. "I never would have suspected what was going on with him."

Fortunately, when the hosts of the reception found out about Prentice's situation, they immediately invited him to stay in the guesthouse of their large home. They really didn't know him. They were simply open to helping someone in need—acting out the truth of one of my favorite Bible verses. I've already quoted it once before, but here it is again: "For unto whomsoever much is given, of him shall be much required" (Luke 12:48, KJV).

That verse means a lot to Pat and me because it touches on one of our core values. We believe that those who've been blessed in life should be a blessing to others. We try to teach this philosophy to our children in words and example. It's the impetus behind our nonprofit organization, Pat & Emmitt Smith Charities, which focuses on "unique educational experiences and enrichment opportunities for underserved children" in a number of ways, including support of the Children's Defense Fund. It's also the inspiration for Pat's nonprofit, Treasure You, which she'll tell you about a little later.

A DREAM AND HOW TO ACHIEVE IT

As it turned out, Prentice stayed in that family's guesthouse for the rest of his senior year, so we stayed in touch with this outstanding young man. When he learned that our charity was sponsoring an essay contest for teenagers, he entered it. The assigned theme was "My Lifetime Dream and How I Plan to Achieve It." What Prentice wrote told us a lot about how remarkable he is.

Prentice wrote in his essay that he "grew up in a low-income neighborhood, facing obstacles on a daily basis." He struggled through elementary and middle school with little support or encouragement from his parents and finally decided to leave his negative home environment at the age of fifteen. For more than three years, until he was offered quarters in the family's guest-house, he often slept on friends' sofas and sometimes in his car.

In his essay, Prentice wrote that he wanted a better life and wanted, ultimately, to "influence the world for good." His difficult experiences and challenges made him determined to pursue his dream of becoming a police chief. He was pursuing that dream by excelling in his studies and becoming active in his community despite his homeless status.

This teen, without a family to support him, volunteered as a youth-basketball coach and was named coach of the year in his league. His community center manager offered this praise: "Prentice talked to the kids like he was twenty-five years old. He had an amazing wisdom and coaching ability for a fourteen-year-old."

Prentice also wrote in his essay that "achieving academically is the foundation for succeeding." This teenager without any family support earned good grades due to his perseverance and discipline.

I liked the fact that Prentice, like me, was goal oriented. He outlined his success strategy, which included surrounding himself with positive role models and mentors and using athletics as a means of motivation through rough times. Thanks to his CDF scholarship, Prentice was set to attend Texas A&M University– Commerce, where he planned on playing football and majoring in criminal justice. And he was already taking thoughtful steps toward his career goal by serving as a director for the Dallas Police Athletic League, a crime-prevention program that tries to inspire young people through sports activities.

You might have guessed by now that Prentice won our essay competition. Did I mention that the grand prize was an invitation to accompany my family and me to Canton, Ohio, for all the events surrounding my induction into the Pro Football Hall of Fame? Prentice was allowed to bring a guest, so he brought his career mentor and role model, Officer Billy Middleton of the

Dallas Independent School District Police and Security Services department. Prentice and Officer Middleton attended my induction ceremony and speech as well as the private VIP celebration afterward, where they met Jerry Jones, Michael Irvin, Troy Aikman, Eric Dickerson, Mark Stepnoski, and Roger Staubach.

"Hanging out with Emmitt and his family, hearing the speeches by the Hall of Fame inductees, and the whole experience is something I will never forget," Prentice said later.

In my Hall of Fame induction speech, I said, "There's a difference between merely having a dream and fulfilling a vision. Most people only dream." I'm proud to say that Prentice is still dreaming and working hard to fulfill his vision. Pat and I have stayed in touch with him. The former homeless teen is now a resident adviser in his college dorm, helping guide other students through their college years.

In addition to Prentice, Pat and I have become mentors for two other young people who were recipients of the CDF's Beat the Odds scholarships: Julie Negussie and Jasmine Gibson. We were so impressed with these three young people that we decided to sponsor our own scholarship in 2011. This recipient's name is Ja'Mesha Morgan. She comes from a single-parent home in Dallas, and when her mother lost her job, Ja'Mesha and her brother took on jobs in the neighborhood to help support the family. Somehow Ja'Mesha still managed to be ranked first academically in her class at South Oak Cliff High School. She wants to pursue a doctorate in psychology and hopes to work with adopted children and children in the foster care system one day.

INVESTING IN DREAMS

Pat and I believe that one of the greatest gifts you can give someone is the opportunity for a college education. Since 1998 we have donated twenty-three scholarships through the Take Stock in Children program near my hometown in Escambia County, Florida. The scholarship program is run by the Escambia County Public Schools Foundation. My mother, Mary, serves on their board of directors, so I know they run a tight ship there!

I consider Prentice, Julie, Jasmine, Ja'Mesha, and the twenty-three Take Stock in Children scholarship recipients we've sponsored to be part of our family, but they are also an investment that will pay off in big ways. Pat and I tell our scholarship students that we are providing them with the opportunity to obtain a higher education and to do great things in their lives, but we also want them to pass on our gift by accepting the responsibility to one day turn back and extend a hand to someone else.

We have invested in their success, and we are already seeing dividends as the first of the group begin to graduate. One young woman has graduated from seminary, and another is entering law school. We love hearing from them—and we hear from them often. Even the young men who have attended my football camps over the years stay in touch and give thanks for their experiences. To hear about the positive impact we've had on their lives is a wonderful gift.

Among those who have personally thanked me for their football-camp experiences is LaDainian Tomlinson, the all-pro running back for the New York Jets. LaDainian, who is known as L.T., grew up in Waco, Texas, and was a big Cowboys fan. He told me that attending my football camp and meeting me helped nurture his vision to play professional football. I can't think of any greater accomplishment than to do that for someone. And to have such a great young man list me as one of his inspirations is, as they say in the MasterCard commercials, *priceless*.

Helping underserved young students access higher education is one of the primary goals of Pat & Emmitt Smith Charities, but we strive to do more than provide scholarships. We also offer young people educational experiences to expand their vision and fuel their dreams. We want to be mentors and encouragers, so we try to stay in personal contact with the recipients of our charitable efforts. Pat and I both had angels in our lives who stepped up and reached out to provide experiences that expanded our vision for what was possible in our own lives. We want to do the same now that we've been so blessed.

Daniel Pipkin is another young man we've been honored to assist in building a vision for his life. I met Daniel several years ago when I was touring and speaking at Clay Academy, a school run by The Potter's House church. He was a freshman in high school and president of the student body, so he was my tour guide. When we were checking out the school library, I asked the reporters following us to turn off their recorders and cameras for a minute. I then asked Daniel to share his thoughts on what Clay Academy's students needed to make their academic experiences more complete.

I thought Daniel might suggest a new computer lab, laptops for every student, possibly even a new swimming pool or tennis court. Instead, he said something very interesting: "Exposure."

"What do you mean exactly?" I asked. "What type of exposure?"

Daniel then explained that most of the students at Clay Academy had very limited exposure to the world beyond the Dallas area.

"For example," he said. "I have this dream of going to New York City and walking across the floor of the New York Stock Exchange. I've always wanted to see and hear what it is really like there."

Daniel's suggestion really caught my interest. Pat and I have both noticed that it is difficult for many young people to dream beyond what they've experienced. They can see things on televisions or in movies, but unless they've had firsthand exposure, they often have trouble accepting that what they dream can become their reality.

After Daniel told me of his dream, I thought for a few seconds and remembered a contact I'd just made at the New York Stock Exchange. I still had his card in my wallet, in fact. So after a slight pause, I told the young man, "We can make that happen."

Thanks to some friends in the right places, Pat and I sent Daniel and his entire class of thirteen students to New York City, where they walked the floor of the New York Stock Exchange, attended a performance of *The Lion King* on Broadway, toured the United Nations and the top floor of the Empire State Building, and visited the National September 11 Memorial at Ground Zero, which many students said was a very emotional and educational experience.

"We saw it as a reminder of the pain and suffering there, and why we need to always be thankful and never take for granted our freedom," Daniel said.

Pat and I were glad to help expand the vision of all those students and especially Daniel, a dynamic young man whom I was proud to recommend in his application to Brown University. He is now a student at Brown, with a vision so grand that he's majoring in international relations with a focus on political and economic issues and global wealth management. We're very proud of Daniel and all the students we've encouraged.

It touches our hearts to hear the stories told by our young friends assisted through our charities. It's one thing to write a check to help others, but even more rewarding to build long-term relationships and have a lasting impact on their lives by guiding and mentoring them.

NEED A BLESSING? BE A BLESSING!

Pat and I have discovered that there is great healing power in giving back to others. Doing good things for others lifts us up physically, mentally, and spiritually.

With that in mind, sometimes when I feel drained by all the demands on my time in my business activities, I'll call or visit our staff at Pat & Emmitt Smith Charities and ask them what they have for me to do. They may send me to help with a toy delivery or on a surprise visit to a hospital, school, children's home, or senior center. Those trips always invigorate me and lift my spirits.

I'm often asked to speak before large groups and to participate in big charity events with a lot of media present, but I really enjoy the opportunity to quietly slip in and work alongside our staff and other volunteers without a lot of commotion. That's why I can honestly tell you that there is no better feeling than doing something simply to make a difference in the lives of others.

Before Christmas in 2010, we had a charity party and toy drive for St. Philip's Community Center, which serves needy families in South Dallas. The day after the party, our charities executive director, Dr. Lara Ashmore, told me she would be delivering the toys the next morning. I asked if I could tag along.

Lara and I drove to South Dallas the next morning. I got to play Santa Claus, and I got in a pretty good workout, too. I helped unload the toys from the truck and then stayed for two hours visiting with the students at the school that is part of the community center. This was right after my trip to Benin for the *Who Do You Think You Are?* television show, and I shared our experiences there with the students during my surprise visit. Some of them suggested that I return as a substitute teacher because we'd had so much fun.

Stepping outside your bubble and putting aside your own concerns and challenges to help others is a wonderful form of therapy. But to tell you the truth, I'm a slacker compared to Pat, who is a true Hall of Famer when it comes to taking her need for a blessing and turning it around so that she becomes a blessing. I'll step aside here and let Pat tell you a great story of doing just that.

PAT SMITH'S TREASURE YOU

Pat: The work that Emmitt and I do with Pat & Emmitt Smith Charities is very rewarding, and we both enjoy it. Frankly, though,

I wanted to do something on my own to make a difference. Being married to Emmitt is wonderful. He's a great man. But as an independent woman with her own dreams and goals, I wanted to make my own mark.

I'd always been successful in school. At James Madison University, I was president of the student government and home-coming queen, too. When Emmitt and I married, each of us already had a child of our own, and then I had three more in quick succession. I love all of our children, of course. I wouldn't change a thing about our blended family, which is very harmonious and loving. But when Emmitt went dancing off and became the *Dancing with the Stars* champion, I felt a little left out. We had a ball during the competition, but Cheryl was my husband's dancing partner and, honestly, as his wife I wanted to be out there with him instead. I love dancing with that man!

Aside from that, Emmitt's long list of achievements, including his induction into the Hall of Fame, stirred up my desire to leave a legacy of my own. Emmitt isn't the only competitor in our family. I had been Miss Virginia USA, and I was first runner-up in the Miss USA contest. And if you don't think those contests are competitive, I can tell you stories to convince you otherwise!

I was yearning to do something, but I wasn't sure what to do. So I prayed, and God placed a plan in my heart and mind. He guided me to play a bigger game by helping other women. After my mother died, I created a charity to provide mental health care for women in need. When I was just twenty-two years old, my mother passed away from breast cancer. I missed her terribly and still do. But I was very lucky to have several other women mentor me and guide me in the years that followed—they acted as my angels in my mother's absence. I decided to call my charity Page's Angels since my mother's middle name was Page. Page's Angels is just beginning its work, but my goal is to do for others what those angels did for me in my time of need.

I am also reaching out to help others through a business organization called Treasure You. The idea for this came to me when I heard a sermon in which Bishop Jakes talked about listening to God's calling on us. Bishop Jakes said if there is something stirring us to action, we should always pay attention and respond.

I often feel as if Bishop Jakes is talking directly to me in his sermons. This time, it was as if he were sitting next to me in the church and speaking to my heart. He inspired me to act on a thought that had been circulating in my mind for a few weeks based on conversations with my female friends.

So many women I know neglect their own interests and even their own physical and emotional health because they are focused on their relationships and their family duties. The thought that kept coming back to me is that women need to value themselves, make the most of their gifts, and see themselves as treasures to be shared in a larger context.

We all want to be fulfilled, fully engaged, and appreciated for our gifts. The person who feels valued for her gifts is also happier and more fun to be around. As Emmitt likes to say, "If Mama ain't happy, ain't nobody happy!"

To fulfill my dream of helping other women create their own happiness, I hosted a Treasure You retreat for eighteen women married to high-profile men from the world of business, sports, politics, entertainment, and religion. We met in Arizona to take the first steps toward creating a community of women to share each other's dreams, passions, fears, and insecurities. The results and response were so great that I've been inspired to conduct similar retreats for women across the country. I've also taped several television shows created for the purpose of inspiring women by telling the stories of great ladies like Cookie Johnson, wife of Earvin "Magic" Johnson.

I've been so blessed to have supportive women in my life who have nurtured me and pushed me to pursue my passions and purpose. I want to encourage women from all walks of life to do the same. In helping them, I'm fulfilling my dream of making a mark and leaving a legacy.

MULTIPLY YOUR BLESSINGS

Emmitt: I'm back! (You give a woman a little space in your book, and she tries to take over!)

Actually, my beautiful and intelligent—and yes, competitive— wife inspires me, and I hope she inspires you to get more involved in helping others. You don't have to be wealthy to do it. You don't have to have a lot of free time. There are as many ways of helping as there are individuals.

Too often people put off giving back or reaching out by using the excuse that they'll wait until they've reached financial security or until they retire and have more time. I have to admit that earlier in my life, I used those same excuses. But the truth is that you can be a blessing to others at every stage of life and in many different ways.

We sometimes lock into the idea that giving back has to involve making a big financial contribution to a charity or nonprofit service organization, but that is only one method of helping others. Giving your time and your talents and your knowledge can mean just as much or even more than signing a check. The Chinese proverb still holds true: "Give a man a fish, and you feed him for a day. Teach a man to fish, and you feed him for a lifetime."

Sharing your life's experience with others is one of the best gifts you can give them. Young people benefit from hearing how you made it and also about the mistakes you made along the way. Describing your failures and how you overcame them can save others valuable time and effort in their own lives and careers. It can be every bit as valuable as financial support.

And don't forget the possibilities of hands-on volunteer service. On Martin Luther King Jr. Day in 2010, Pat and I took our kids to Congo Street in the Jubilee Park neighborhood of South Dallas. Early in its history, the sixty-two-block neighborhood was very upscale, with fine old homes, but then it became run down and dangerous with drug dealers and prostitutes. Now there is a major effort by the city to issue grants to revitalize the neighborhood, renovate homes, and bring that area back as a safe and comfortable place to live.

Pat and the kids and I took part in a day of service on Martin Luther King Jr.'s birthday. We joined architect Brent Brown, who has been renovating homes one by one in that neighborhood. Donating our time on that special day to a community that needs a helping hand was a great experience for our entire family and a good lesson for our kids. They saw that some people are less fortunate and, like me, grew up without a lot of things that they have now.

My message to them is to be thankful for their blessings but to know that someday they will have to earn their own way. We also encourage them to be humble enough to help raise up those around them.

Some of those volunteering alongside us were volunteers with AmeriCorps. This government agency, similar to the Peace Corps, offers more than seventy-five thousand opportunities each year for volunteers who want to share their time and talents. AmeriCorps works with a network of local and national nonprofit groups in communities across the country. Its volunteers tutor and mentor disadvantaged youth, fight illiteracy, improve health services, build affordable housing, teach computer skills, clean parks and streams, manage or operate after-school programs, and respond to disasters. Another great benefit in volunteering for this organization is that full-time volunteers who complete their service agreement earn a Segal AmeriCorps Education Award of $4,725 to help pay for college or graduate school or to pay back qualified student loans. Some even receive a modest living allowance during their term of service.

AmeriCorps (www.americorps.gov) is part of the Corporation for National and Community Service (www.nationalservice.gov), which puts to work more than five million American volunteers through its core programs—Senior Corps, AmeriCorps, and Learn and Serve America—while also leading President Obama's national call-to-service initiative, United We Serve.

Our family worked on Congo Street with thirty-five AmeriCorps volunteers to rehabilitate and weatherize two houses that will benefit low-income families. The kids painted while I helped repair roofs, install kitchen cabinets and countertops, and put in insulation. I was hoping to impress the kids with my professional construction know-how. But to tell the truth, they were having way too much fun painting to care what I was doing!

SHARING YOUR TIME AND TALENT

To match your own talents and interests to volunteer positions, you can go to helpful websites like philanthropy.com, which covers the world of giving, and volunteermatch.org, which has connected more than five million volunteers to programs needing them, sometimes at a rate of sixty-three per hour nationwide.

Here are some time- and talent-sharing ideas if you are looking for opportunities to make a difference in the lives of others. (Most of these organizations won't turn down a check either.)

- *The American Red Cross (www.redcross.org).* This great group always needs volunteers for its many activities, including disaster response, blood drives, youth outreach, fund drives, and special events. They even have volunteer positions for computer-savvy people and those who can sew and knit.

- *The Salvation Army (www.salvationarmyusa.org).* This faith-based organization enlists volunteers for a wide range of programs including disaster relief, community centers, youth camps, elderly services, League of Mercy, and Christmas charities.

- *Habitat for Humanity (www.habitat.org).* This home-building nonprofit has volunteer programs in most midsize to large communities in the United States and around the world. This great organization offers youth programs for students, teachers, and youth group leaders and members; special women's work teams; and RV "Care-A-Vanners" and "A Brush with Kindness" programs to revitalize neighborhoods and maintain the exteriors of Habitat homes.

- *Make-A-Wish Foundation (www.wish.org).* Children dealing with medical problems and their families have so many challenges. This nonprofit needs volunteers for everything from language translation to transportation and fundraising.

- *Local soup kitchens.* I've known people who've benefited greatly from taking time out from dealing with their own challenges to serve meals to others with even greater burdens. You can find your local soup kitchens online or through your church.

- *Local hospitals and public nursing homes.* Volunteers in these facilities do everything from answering phones at the switchboard to helping patients get around to supporting the staff and delivering meals, flowers, and other gifts.

- *Schools and libraries.* So many teachers are overworked and overwhelmed in public schools and private schools alike. Many welcome volunteer classroom aides, cafeteria servers, and playground monitors. Some parents find this is a great way to be involved in their children's and grandchildren's schools while serving the community and enjoying the company of young people. Libraries, too, are often short staffed and welcome volunteer help.

- *Your church.* Nearly all churches big and small rely on volunteers to assist the pastor during services as well as with youth groups, services for the elderly, Bible study, Sunday school, fundraising, missionary trips, and community outreach projects. If your church doesn't have the program you'd like, why not volunteer to start one?

MULTIPLY YOUR BLESSINGS

Whatever you achieve in life—accomplishments, material possessions, wealth, prestige—all of it means very little when you are gone. It is what you've done for others that determines your legacy. Your contributions to the greater good will define you. How many lives will you have touched? How many will say that your departure is their loss and the world's as well?

My minister, spiritual guide, and friend Bishop Jakes has reinforced my sense of community responsibility and encouraged me. He reminds me often that the glory for everything we do is God's because he guides us all on his path. I've also learned that the more you give to God and to others, the more blessings you receive.

I live in gratitude for the blessings I've received because I am aware that one injury, one mistake in judgment, one twist of fate could have changed my life dramatically. I know that without God's grace I would not be in the position I am in today, and I believe that one of my chief responsibilities is to help others help themselves.

My football days are behind me now. They were glorious, but they are not my glory days. My glory days are still to come. I've just begun my days of giving. Pat and I are just warming up in our efforts to reach out.

They say timing is everything, and our timing could not be better because the world of philanthropy is rapidly changing thanks to new technologies and innovative approaches to giving. Within just a few days of the 2010 earthquake in Haiti, for example, Americans donated more than $22 million to the American Red Cross relief efforts simply by sending a text message and approving a ten-dollar contribution. At one point, donations were flowing in at the rate of $500,000 an hour!

Whatever you achieve in life—accomplishments, material possessions, wealth, prestige—all of it means very little when you are gone. It is what you've done for others that determines your legacy. Your contributions to the greater good will define you. How many lives will you have touched? How many will say that your departure is their loss and the world's as well?

Now there are no excuses. Everyone can make a difference. Everyone can pitch in, whether it's investing money or sharing your time and talents to help others develop their own gifts. Proverbs 11:25 says,

A generous person will prosper;
  whoever refreshes others will be refreshed.

I believe that whatever you give will come back to you tenfold. Pat and I have realized this time and again. The satisfaction we've received from our giving has touched our souls, and it has taught our children lessons they will never forget.

My father once said that he was more proud of what I'd done in the community than anything I'd accomplished on the football field. Dad doesn't say much, but he sure has a way of getting to me. I'm glad to give whatever I can to those in need. After all, the Salvation Army sponsored my first football team in the peewee league, and look what that meant to my life. I know from experience how important it is to reach out and lift up others at every opportunity.

The Salvation Army motto is "Heart to God, Hand to man." I try to live that motto, and I encourage you to do the same. Reach out to others in whatever way you can because when you help others, you create a ripple effect that makes the world a better place for everyone.

The clock is running, and the game of life is in play. Are you ready to dream . . . and to make those dreams a reality? Today is the day to embrace the life God has called you to. Game on!

ACKNOWLEDGMENTS

I'VE DISCOVERED THAT even though it's not quite as physically punishing as playing football, publishing a book still requires a big team. I'd like to thank all my book team members, beginning with my literary agents, Jan Miller Rich and Nena Madonia, and the entire squad at Tyndale House Publishers, including Maria Eriksen, Stephanie Voiland, Carol Traver, Anne Christian Buchanan, Lisa Jackson, Jackie Nuñez, and Jon Farrar.

My business manager, Werner Scott, and my executive assistants, Kris Tyler and Kari Rusco, were instrumental in this publishing project.

A special thanks goes out to Wes Smith, who provided a great service in drawing out my stories and putting my words on the page. Thanks also to my speechwriter and speaking coach, Arthur Samuel Joseph, for his suggestions and assistance.